Praise for *Words from the Window Seat*

"Beautiful, insightful, ⟨...⟩ Taylor has nailed it in this b⟨...⟩ of the right words being give⟨...⟩ time and invites us to be th⟨...⟩ way by the boatload."

—BOB GOFF, *NEW YORK TIMES* BESTSELLING AUTHOR OF
LOVE DOES; *EVERYBODY, ALWAYS*; AND *DREAM BIG*

"*Words from the Window Seat* is an on-time companion for the traveler at heart. Taylor Tippett shares beautifully honest experiences and insights gathered from her life—including life as a flight attendant. These pages will empower you to explore the many opportunities we have each day to encounter light and share love with others while traveling. Whether traveling by air or traveling through life. This book is an encouragement to be present in the everyday, no matter what comes your way."

—MORGAN HARPER NICHOLS, AUTHOR OF
ALL ALONG YOU WERE BLOOMING

"Reading *Words from the Window Seat* feels like snuggling up next to the most empathic friend, who reminds you of all that's so beautiful and right with you and the world. These words feel like a deep exhale, a remembering."

—RUTHIE LINDSEY, SPEAKER AND AUTHOR OF *THERE I AM:
THE JOURNEY FROM HOPELESSNESS TO HEALING*

"Taylor is a radiant light, and her stories leave a wake of love on this earth."

—JEDIDIAH JENKINS, AUTHOR OF *TO SHAKE THE
SLEEPING SELF* AND *LIKE STREAMS TO THE OCEAN*

"*Words from the Window Seat* is basically a long conversation over coffee with Taylor. It's authentic, lighthearted and honest, fun and funny, serious when it needs to be, and just all-around feels like a big hug from a good friend. If you've ever felt lost, wondered if you're getting it 'right,' struggled with anxiety or depression, been burdened with grief or fear, or questioned how your life was going to turn out—you aren't going to want to miss this down-to-earth, encouraging page-turner from Taylor."

—ALLISON FALLON, AUTHOR OF
THE POWER OF WRITING IT DOWN

words
from
the
window
seat

words from the window seat

The Everyday Magic of Kindness, Courage, and Being Your True Self

TAYLOR TIPPETT

NELSON
BOOKS

An Imprint of Thomas Nelson

Words from the Window Seat

© 2021 by Taylor Tippett

Published in Nashville, Tennessee, by Nelson Books, an imprint of Thomas Nelson. Nelson Books and Thomas Nelson are registered trademarks of HarperCollins Christian Publishing, Inc.

Published in association with literary agent Tawny Johnson of Illuminate Literary Agency, www.illluminateliterary.com.

Thomas Nelson titles may be purchased in bulk for educational, business, fundraising, or sales promotional use. For information, please email SpecialMarkets@ThomasNelson.com.

Any internet addresses, phone numbers, or company or product information printed in this book are offered as a resource and are not intended in any way to be or to imply an endorsement by Thomas Nelson, nor does Thomas Nelson vouch for the existence, content, or services of these sites, phone numbers, companies, or products beyond the life of this book.

Some names and identifying factors have been changed to protect the privacy of those who have shared their stories.

Illustrations by Joseph Tilley and Taylor Tippett.

Library of Congress Cataloging-in-Publication Data

Names: Tippett, Taylor, 1993- author.
Title: Words from the window seat : the everyday magic of kindness, courage, and being your true self / by Taylor Tippett.
Description: Nashville : Thomas Nelson, 2021. | Summary: "Taylor Tippett, known as the flight attendant who leaves encouraging notes on passenger windows, shares how readers can find encouragement and meaning amid the brokenness of this world as they learn to recognize the magic of small moments, the power of everyday kindnesses, and the beauty found in every person's unique story"-- Provided by publisher.
Identifiers: LCCN 2021007782 (print) | LCCN 2021007783 (ebook) | ISBN 9781400225378 (trade paperback) | ISBN 9781400225385 (epub)
Subjects: LCSH: Encouragement--Religious aspects--Christianity.
Classification: LCC BV4647.E53 T57 2021 (print) | LCC BV4647.E53 (ebook) | DDC 248.4--dc23
LC record available at https://lccn.loc.gov/2021007782
LC ebook record available at https://lccn.loc.gov/2021007783

Printed in the United States of America

21 22 23 24 25 LSC 10 9 8 7 6 5 4 3 2 1

My story of becoming is spread out on these next pages you are about to turn and dive into. Before you do, I have to dedicate this whole thing. Talk about my worst nightmare. I want to dedicate it to my dog, my husband, Santa Claus, God, and to my favorite Trader Joe's cashier. This book is for and because of so many beautiful humans. It has roots. How do I scoop this all up and give my love to every single last one of you?

I think about my six-year-old self. I am dedicating these next few pages to her. I hope she knows how loved she was, even when she couldn't feel it. I know she would be so proud of the woman I have turned out to be. It's for your six-year-old self too. Go back and talk to them sometime. They may need it more than you know.

This is for every last sunset, sunrise, sidewalk crack, wildflower, stranger, and black cup of coffee that made me fall deeper in love with God and become a lot more like Love.

To anyone who has called heartache, loss, sadness, heaviness, depression, anxiety, or pain a friend. These next pages are yours. May you never forget how loved, valuable, and important you are.

This is for you. For *all* of you. All my love.

contents

introduction

a cotton-candy, bright-orange-and-pink, out-of-this-world sunset was staring at me outside my window. I was sitting in my special flight attendant jump seat on an airplane getting ready to touch down in Chicago. Sitting there in front of all my passengers, I couldn't help but cry. That kind of beauty just does stuff to my insides. Without even thinking about it, my hand went up over my heart so I could silently give thanks and soak it all up.

As I was sitting there with my hand over my heart, just taking it all in, the landing gear popped down, startling me like it always does. I got to thinking how the landing gear comes down at a specific altitude, usually when the airplane goes under two thousand feet. It doesn't pop down at an altitude of five thousand feet or an altitude of five hundred feet but exactly when we dip below two thousand feet in the air. The pilots never put down the airplane's landing gear too early, and they for sure never drop the landing gear too late. I don't think any of us would want to be on a plane that puts its landing gear down too late. But somewhere in the midst of all the button pressing and airplane landing, there is a sweet spot. A spot where it is safe to let the gears down, land, and come right on back home.

I believe that our stories work in the same way—at least mine has. In 2014, at one of the worst possible stages of my life, I ripped a piece of paper off of a dollar-store notebook, wrote down a life lesson shortened into a tiny sentence with a black Sharpie, and grabbed some tape from an airplane cart. I hung the piece of paper on a window inside the airplane, snapped a quick picture, and decided to tuck the paper into the seat-back pocket in hopes that someone who really needed to read those words would find it. I wanted to "pay it forward," passing along a piece of something that had inspired me while traveling, meeting new humans, and growing into myself. It was a decision that would shape the way I view kindness and the magic of small moments. This is how my project, Words from the Window Seat, was born.

Bits and pieces of my story have snuck out in Instagram captions, blog posts, and podcasts; over cups of coffee with strangers; and on little pieces of paper I've hung up on airplane windows. But I'm finally putting them all in one place, and I'm really excited to share the complete stories with you. I want my stories to be ones you can hold on to when life seems unbearable. When you experience heartache for the first time or the fiftieth time. When you have to dig deep and remember that joy is out there waiting for you. We are all searching, growing, beautiful walking stories who need encouragement.

Each chapter in this book shares the story behind a note I left for a passenger to find. Some stories are old, and some are new. As I share my travels, struggles, and growth with you, I hope you'll see God in a fresh, beautiful new way in your own world. I hope these stories spark within you a deep desire to practice kindness and courage every day, in ways big or small.

While reading this book, imagine you and I are sitting next to each other toward the back of the airplane on a flight. It's one of those really lucky flights where no one is sitting in the middle seat. Oh yeah; we are going to Paris, too, because a fresh croissant and a walk under the Eiffel Tower sound like a dream come true right about now. It's just me and you, two strangers sharing stories.

i never really believed in magic—at least not before I took my first airplane ride. The magic and joy that come from flying on an airplane is very rare and special. Did you know there is a specific time of day that holds the most magic while flying? I think so, at least, and you could say I'm kinda an expert with all the traveling I do. The most magical time to be on an airplane is around six in the morning, right when the morning sun is stretching its arms up over the sky to say hello to us. I know six in the morning sounds like a punishment, but trust me, being in the air at this time is unlike anything I've experienced. I'm sure you have seen a sunrise from the ground, but seeing one from thirty thousand feet in the sky is something different.

I can think back to one specific, magical six-in-the-morning flight I was working in 2014 that has stuck with me. I had been a flight attendant for three months at that point, and I was still getting used to the job. I was still pronouncing city names horribly wrong. I was still overly nervous to pour Diet Cokes, which is by far the hardest drink to pour on an airplane (just in case I poured a little too much and gave a passenger a spill they didn't ask for). I was learning so much, especially how to be kind to the strangers I had daily encounters with: passengers on my flights, coworkers, humans in airports, drivers in hotel vans, and all the other places in between.

Being a flight attendant is stretching because it requires that you interact with strangers, who in most cases are so stressed from all that happens when traveling, that they are sometimes the worst versions of themselves by the time I greet them on the plane. Waiting in line at the ticket counters, TSA pat downs, dealing with agents, gate changes, seven-dollar bottles of water, checking their luggage when they didn't want to check their luggage, and all the other things they encounter at the airport can be really hard. If I try to help someone fit their bag in the overhead bin and it doesn't fit, it's my fault, even though I didn't make the bins or buy the bag that wasn't the right size. If I ask someone to get off of their phone during the safety demonstration, I'm the bad guy, even though the safety demonstration is the most important part of the whole journey. Usually, I have to ask them multiple times, too, and that's when things really start to spice up. I wish I could let everyone do whatever makes them the happiest, but that's not always in the safety and best interest of everyone else around. It can be a lot.

I was learning how to be kind to not the kindest of humans. I was being stretched like a rubber band. I found myself, more often than not, annoyed and losing empathy when dealing with the hardest people to love. I was really discouraged. I was learning a lot, but the lessons felt stale. The inner work of becoming the most beautiful, kind, patient version of myself—the version I deeply desired and wanted to become—wasn't sticking. Something was off.

During that specific morning flight, I had just finished a quick beverage service and was sitting in the back of a Boeing 737. It was a fairly empty flight where the few passengers on it were sleeping—some even snoring with their eyes closed tight. As I was sipping on my coffee, I started thinking about my own personal life away from work and traveling. I believe that we become like the things we love, and if I'm being honest, I didn't love a lot of good, healthy things. The things I found myself loving were toxic relationships and behaviors, holding on to pain, impatience, self-doubt, and not handling my mental health very well. How could I ever expect to love others well if the love I had in my life and toward myself was so unhealthy? How could I build people up if I only tore myself down? How could I be kind to others if I wasn't first being kind to myself?

That last question really shook me. I became a flight attendant so I could be a reflection of the kindness I so freely received because of God's love. I wanted to be Love in the world. When I say *Love* here and when you see it used throughout this book, I want you to know that I mean it as being like Jesus. I like referring to Jesus as Love because this is what Jesus is to me and what Jesus calls us to be as well. I also want to create room for those who may not know him or may not be comfortable using his name. Everyone is invited and welcomed here. We are all striving to become better and to look a lot more like Love.

I'd signed up to love others when it wasn't convenient. But I suddenly realized that because of my lack of self-growth and inward kindness, I was failing daily. Wasn't I supposed to put on my own oxygen mask before helping others put on theirs?

I needed to start that inner work. I needed a pep talk. I needed encouragement. I had to write all of this down in my notebook. I journaled about how unhappy I was at the current time in my life. I needed to love myself with more kindness and confidence so that I could heal and become healthy. I had a life-altering realization before the sun was even fully awake—as I said, there's just something magical about a six o'clock flight. I took a deep breath and read over my words. It was a beautiful place to start.

As I went to put away my journal in my flight attendant bag, I saw a tiny notepad sticking out that I'd received from graduating flight attendant training. I honestly have no idea why I kept it, but I'm so thankful I did. My dollar-store notepad was my first lesson about the magic of little moments. I can't really tell you why, but something sparked inside of me seeing it. I wanted to let people in on what I was learning, as I was learning it. Not after I had already been through my inner work but while I was in the thick of it.

I couldn't help but think about all the other humans out there who could be struggling with their own short-comings. What if my early morning revelation that I needed to be kinder to myself was exactly what someone else needed to hear today too? *How could my words be used to change the course of someone's day, or even life?* I wondered. *What if I started leaving notes of encouragement on random flights for someone to find?* I could learn to embody Love in the midst of someone else's ordinary day through an act of kindness as small as a piece of paper. An idea was being born.

With a Sharpie, I wrote down the words I had just written in my journal a few minutes before. "Be kind to yourself." As I looked at the finished product, I started thinking bigger. What if I took this idea even further and shared my notes online before I tucked them in a seat-back pocket for someone else to find? I had always been one to share vulnerability on the internet, but this felt different. So, before I even had time to think about what I was doing, I taped the note on an airplane window, snapped a picture, and then left the note in the seat-back pocket for a stranger to find.

I'm not quite sure what happened to that first note and who it was meant for, but I do know how much it touched a whole bunch of people online after I posted the picture. I received a flood of direct messages and emails right after my post went up. There were a lot of "me too's" and strangers sharing how they were practicing being kind to themselves. So maybe my note was for the person who sat in that seat that day, but it was also for a whole bunch of other humans.

We all have moments where we need encouragement. (I wish I could wear a Bluetooth earpiece where someone could secretly feed me encouragement and love all day long.) We all forget to be kind to ourselves—I for one am not my own best cheerleader. It's really easy to push ourselves as hard as we can, and it's even easier to beat ourselves up when we fail. It's hard to practice kindness toward yourself, but it's hard work that is worth doing. Being kind to ourselves can open us up to a whole new world filled with kindness, courage, and a little bit of magic. And that world ends up impacting a lot of other humans around us.

Now when I have internal pep talks and I remind myself, *Be kind to yourself*, I know what the fruit of that looks like. It looks like a beautiful step toward healthiness, which allows me to be healthy with others. It looks like giving myself grace, which then leads to being kind to strangers and having grace with them as well. It looks like small acts of kindness that have the power to embody Love. Kindness looks a lot like Jesus. I hope I continue to look a lot more like that.

O ne summer day in 2013, the TV started whispering that American Airlines was hiring 1,500 flight attendants for the first time in over ten years. When I heard that, I immediately thought back to my early childhood years when I dreamed about what I would be when I got older. Of course there was always the classic list of becoming a teacher, ballerina, astronaut, and all the things most kids dream about, but those quickly faded as I grew up and truly started to figure out who I was and what I was passionate about. I always felt like I wanted to do something different from a really young age.

I remember so clearly one Christmas when my family and I went to visit my grandma, Mimi, in Colorado. I was probably eight years old and was mesmerized by everything in my Mimi's home. She showed me all her gold jewelry and fun scarves, and then she showed me her old flight attendant wings. Mimi started telling me the most amazing stories of when she was a Pan Am flight attendant. I still remember standing in her closet listening to her and watching her face light up. I think that's when the seed was planted of truly wanting to become a flight attendant. I was young, though, and I eventually tucked the dream and the memory with my grandma away.

As I grew up, I thought I wanted to become a marine biologist, and that was my plan once I graduated high school. But even though I had good grades, maintained a great GPA, and was super involved in my high school, I ended up not getting into my dream college that had the best marine biology program, and I was extremely heartbroken. Instead of fighting for my dream career, I started to realize that wasn't what I really wanted to do.

I think most of the time when you are following your dreams, you know you are in the right place when you don't back down for anyone or anything. You keep fighting and pushing for what you want or what you are called to. I didn't fight for my dream of becoming a marine biologist, and that showed me that I needed time to truly think about what I wanted to do and who I wanted to become.

The memory of Mimi's flight attendant stories always lingered in the back of my mind. Here and there I would come back to the dream of becoming a flight attendant, and then one day I sat down with a pen and piece of paper and said, "Okay, Taylor. What do you love, what are you passionate about, who do you want to be, and what do you want to do with your one, beautiful life here on this earth?" I knew I was called to a grand adventure and a different kind of career. I just didn't know how to get there.

This was the part where that news headline came into play and the dream of becoming a flight attendant really started to come to life—it was the little push I had been waiting to receive. I realized that the dream had always been there, ever since I was eight years old, standing wide-eyed in my grandma's closet. Strangely enough, I'd had a phone call with my grandmother a week prior to hearing that American Airlines was hiring so many flight attendants, and we had talked about me maybe wanting to pursue becoming a flight attendant. Some people might call that a coincidence, but I call it purpose. I can just picture God winking at me as I saw that headline spread before my eyes.

My insides started racing. My palms started to sweat. Following my dream to become a flight attendant felt like laying a lot of insecurities down. I'm really bad at committing to things. Dreams, football teams, apartments to live in. Maybe it's the fear of being stuck. Maybe it's the fear of failing. It's probably a combination of a lot of different things. Deciding on my career felt like all of my insecurities were out in the open because I was committing to something so big. I knew I couldn't run once I said "this is what I am choosing." I knew I had to follow through, and I just hoped I was enough. Putting ourselves out there to do things that feel so much bigger than ourselves is a hard thing to do. It is scary and filled with courage and growth. Becoming a flight attendant and following my purpose felt like choosing courage and silencing fear. I was going to pick courage no matter how uncomfortable it felt.

After hearing the news, I ran as fast as I could to my computer. I was going to try my absolute best to become a flight attendant. I polished up my résumé and submitted it to American Airlines. A few weeks later, I heard back and had a Skype interview. A month later I was sitting in first class headed to Dallas, Texas, after staying up all night watching makeup tutorials for my in-person interview. A month after that I was flying back to Dallas to have a physical and a medical test. And just a few weeks after that, the email I had been waiting to receive for six months sat in my inbox. The dates to my training class were staring right at me through my computer screen. I was finally offered a job, as long as I finished my eight weeks of flight attendant training. I was becoming a flight attendant. I had done it. I couldn't shake this feeling of wanting to do the scary things. Dreams felt scary. Failing felt scary. Courage to get up and do the work felt scary, but I just kept showing up with my palms open, asking if God would keep helping me choose courage—and that's exactly what happened.

The time had come to pack my bags and head to training in the new year of 2014, and I was ecstatic. I had never been to Texas for more than a few hours before I moved there for flight attendant training. I had also never lived in a hotel before, and trust me, it's not like they make it seem in the movies. The child in me thought the experience would be exactly like in *Home Alone 2*, and let me tell you something, it was not. All sixty of my classmates were packed tight into the hotel, and we ran the place. I ended up having the best roommate named Toolie, and she was a blessing to spend three months with.

On the first day of class, we put on our red lipstick, slicked back our hair, and headed to the flight attendant training center. We received goodie bags and a tour of where we would spend everyday learning about our new career. There were even snack tables filled with candy and chips. I was in heaven; it felt like training was going to be a walk in the park. Any place with free candy and Dr Pepper was the closest thing to joy on this earth. We were introduced to our classmates and the four instructors in charge of teaching us the ins and outs of the job: Liam, Larry, Jill, and Lynne. Even though I had thought training was going to be a breeze, I quickly found out on day one that the next eight weeks were going to be extremely challenging. I was going to have hours of class time learning evacuation drills, memorizing each airplane from top to bottom, learning all kinds of beverage and food services, and becoming proficient in tons of safety protocols while on the job. I quickly realized that flight attendant training is no joke.

I didn't know how many major airports there were

in the world until I had to memorize the name and code for hundreds of them. I remember making little sayings and mnemonic devices to memorize them all for my very first test. (One of my personal favorites is Mickey's Circle Office for Orlando's airport, MCO, because Disney is Orlando's biggest attraction.) After that first test came many others. We used airplane simulators to practice and learn emergency drills—what flight attendants say and do in the unlikely event of a crash on land or over water. We had at least one drill test a week where we had to use exact verbiage to conduct a practice emergency landing. If we said one word wrong, we had one chance to redo the test or else we failed. If we had more than three fails on tests or drills over the course of the eight weeks of training, we got sent home.

My classmates and I spent hours spread out all over the training center, hotel lobby, and each other's rooms studying our hearts out. I remember feeling discouraged early on. I was really struggling with some mental health issues (more on that later) and overwhelmed by how much I had to learn in such a short amount of time. I wasn't necessarily struggling because learning was hard but because there was so much pressure to not fail. There was so much at stake. We woke up most days before the sun rose and had to make sure we were in regulation with our outfits and personal grooming. I felt out of place at first; high heels and red lipstick just didn't feel like me.

There were strict rules about appearance, how we carried ourselves on campus and at the hotel when we weren't in class, and being on time.

The glittery feeling of being in training had worn off quickly, and reality was starting to kick in. It was difficult in the early days of training to keep fighting for my dream of becoming a flight attendant. I had to push hard to cancel out self-doubt and fears in order to remember what I was working toward and where I was headed. When we work hard for our dreams, sometimes our fears work even harder to get us to quit. I realized that when we are called to do something and fear finds us, we can rest assured that we are in the right place, fighting for the right thing. Usually the more fearful we are, the surer we can be that it is the right step.

After failing a test one winter afternoon, I walked outside to take a breath of the brisk Texas air. I closed my eyes and started talking to God about all my fears and the pressure to succeed at training. I wanted to be a flight attendant so badly, and I needed a big hug of peace and some reassurance. I felt a new hope wash over me. The words "remember your courage" slipped out of my mouth before I even knew what I was saying. God had given me an anthem to get me through.

I wrote it down on a slip of yellow paper and stuck it behind the name tag I wore every single day at training. Every time a test overwhelmed me, I looked at the back of my name tag and spoke my truth over my fears. Every time I had to put on my red lipstick and my insecurities told me I wasn't good enough to follow my dreams, I spoke my truth over myself. I remembered my courage every single time I wanted to set it down and pick up fear instead. I was learning that fear wasn't what mattered most. Even though it screamed the loudest during training, what I did and the choices I made while I was afraid were what made me brave. That was courage. So I kept choosing courage again and again, and before I realized it, training was over.

After eight challenging weeks at training, it was *finally* graduation day. I had my bags packed and was soon to set off for my new home in Chicago. I was going to get my brand-new, shiny wings pinned on my uniform. I will never forget the feeling of hearing my name called and walking up onstage. I was officially a flight attendant. I had done it. I had remembered my courage, and it felt good.

When I reflect on the days right after I graduated flight attendant training and I remember how I held tight to my courage, I think about a country girl moving to her first big city. I think about living with a random family in a literal closet I found for rent on craigslist. I think about my first Chicago winter. I think about working in first class for the first time and how scared I was about messing up. I think about the thousands of miles traveled and the people I got to meet and love. I think about people like Winston.

Winston was the sweetest little old man I found hiding out in the bathroom during a flight I was working. I can still picture his tears streaming when I first found him. He introduced himself and promised me he was okay and that I shouldn't be startled. He was a bit out of it and shaken up for a reason he did not want to get into; he just wanted to return to his seat. As he was walking down the airplane aisle, he suddenly turned and headed back toward me and his hiding spot in the bathroom. I looked at Winston, who had even more tears streaming down his face as he told me he did not have it in him to return to his seat. He was embarrassed because he was in the middle of having a panic attack due to his fear of flying. I comforted him in all the ways I knew how. I shared my personal struggles with panic attacks, trying to make him feel better and less alone. Our "me too's" are powerful. Don't ever forget it.

As Winston and I were holding hands and he was calming down, the pilot announced that we were starting to descend and would be landing soon. Winston's eyes widened, and he took a big gulp. He knew what that meant and told me he was sitting at a window seat, which made his fear of flying worse. He asked if I could shuffle a few people around so he could sit in an aisle seat during landing. As I set off to do some seat shuffling, he started waving at me to come back toward the bathroom. I approached him, and he bravely said, "Wait! No! I have overcome so much in my life. If I let this anxiety have the best of me, it will win. I *have* to sit in that window seat for landing. I have to do it. I can do this." Though he was stressed, I couldn't help thinking about how beautiful a human he was. How full of courage he must be.

Standing outside of the bathroom with Winston, watching his tears come and trying to comfort something so familiar that lives inside of me, I wanted to be more like him.

I wanted to have the courage to keep getting up from my mess and sitting in the places I'm fearful of. I can think of so many areas in life, and I'm sure you can too, where I've struggled to have courage. It's really difficult to replace fear with courage in the spaces where we are afraid and hurting, but we must remember how beautiful it is when we do so. What is it for you? Are you fearful of failing? Are you insecure that you aren't good enough to do what you are called to do? I'm with you so, so much. Yet I find it helpful to remember what Jesus said about fear and how he helps us conquer it. He is always with us, so we have nothing at all to worry about. He strengthens us. He helps us. He upholds us when we feel shaky. He provides for us our courage—always.

———————

The places that ache and sting are scary as can be. So, standing outside the bathroom with Winston, I whispered the words I knew best to be true: "Remember your courage, Winston." He smiled big, let go of my hand, and walked back toward his window seat where he landed safely. He even left the plane with a smile.

One thing no one really tells you about becoming a flight attendant is that it takes a lot of time until you make enough money to live comfortably. When I first started the job, I was pretty much making the bare minimum. I also didn't understand the concept of saving money because all I wanted to do was fly all over the place and travel my little heart out. Because of my big desire to travel all over the world after leaving training in Texas, when I was looking for a place to rent in Chicago, my goal was to save as much as possible. All my training friends who were also going to be based in Chicago were from there originally and had homes to stay in already, so I didn't have anyone to team up with to get an apartment. I understood I wasn't going to have a big paycheck to live off of and that I would be home practically never, so when I saw a craigslist ad for a room renting at $300 per month, I went for it. I was still in Texas at the time, finishing up my last days of training, so I didn't have the capability to go see the new spot in person until moving day.

I walked into my new home to meet the sweetest Vietnamese family of three and a Vietnamese foreign exchange student and her boyfriend who lived on the third floor of an old Irving Park home. When I was first shown my room after meeting all my new neighbors, I realized I was going to be living in a big walk-in closet, which the pictures I had seen beforehand hadn't clearly conveyed. It was truly humbling to be in such a small space, yet so beautiful.

I had picked Chicago as my new home because I wanted to start a different kind of life. One I was proud of, where I would take risks and get uncomfortable. I had grown up living outside of a city, with the same opportunities and grocery stores, and I wanted something different. I wanted something big. I wanted to meet lots of new people and experience new things that the suburb life couldn't offer. I was taking big risks and jumping big jumps—doing things that scared me. Living in a closet wasn't ideal, but I thought about the things I would learn from my new environment and my new city. I thought about the places I could travel to because I was saving so much on rent. Do you know what I realized? I was doing it. I was in Chicago and alive and doing the dang thing. It didn't look like what I thought it would. But life rarely does, does it?

I think when we sign up and choose to be like Love, it never looks like what we think it will. Saying yes to Love means getting uncomfortable and letting go of trying to control our own world. It means stepping into the beauty of these small, magical moments. Living in a closet was going to be magical to me because I was going to speak that into life. Sometimes we have to remember to do that. We have to speak life and whimsy over our adventures and dreams, even when they feel like they don't make sense. We have to remember to look at ourselves and say, "You are doing it." We can be proud even when it looks different from what we thought.

———

My new little nook basically had enough space for a twin bed and my books. It also had a corner cutout with a space to hang my clothes and a small little aisle. My room was right in front of the kitchen, which was the source of many mysterious and magnificent smells. My new neighbors often made pho and invited me to eat with them. During my time with them I learned a lot about Asian culture, what it means to open up a home, and the beauty of being close with your family.

At the same time, I was also starting to make other friends who I could go on adventures with. I met a lot of them through the internet, mostly Instagram, which I still think is such an incredible thing. I was shown the best coffee shops, places to eat, and hidden corners of the city that took my breath away. My dream of being a local at a coffee shop—where I could walk in and they would know my order—finally came true. I often found myself walking fifteen minutes down Milwaukee Avenue into my favorite neighborhood in Chicago—Logan Square. There was this Latin spot called Cafe Con Leche that had the best—and I mean *the best*—*cafe con leche*, which is Spanish for coffee with milk. The drinks were the right amount of sweet, the mugs were bigger than your face, and there was something about that particular café that brought the magic to life inside my chest. I felt unstoppable when I sat down and locked eyes with someone there who knew exactly what I was going to order. Feeling known and seen is all we want, isn't it? It lets us know we are valued and important.

I'll never forget my first days as a Chicagoan—finding my secret, not-so-secret spots. A plaza fountain in the heart of downtown became one of my spots. It was next to the huge Chase Tower building, and I stumbled upon it one day as I was exploring my new city. It became a spot of refuge when I was feeling overwhelmed and tied down with stress and anxiety. If you feel this way, too, you should find yourself a secret spot. It can be on your bedroom floor or out in your city or even on the beach; wherever it is, just make sure you hold it close. It's important that we find our secret spots when we can, especially when doing the scary stuff.

As my time in Chicago grew, so did I, learning the ebb and flow of my new life. I figured out how to use the public transportation system and experienced my first real winter. Boy, was that something. I even had some of my first big trips as a flight attendant. I will never forget getting called to work as the lead flight attendant. The lead flight attendant is the one who works first class and kinda runs the show. Crew scheduling called me two hours before I had to show up for the trip to let me know I would be working as the lead, and I was shaking in my boots. I was just coming up on my six-month anniversary of being a flight attendant, and I had avoided working the lead position because it was such a big responsibility. I didn't want to fail. Feeding sixteen people, memorizing each first-class passenger's last name and pronouncing it properly, making all of the announcements, and being in charge of just about everything up front made me so nervous, but I couldn't avoid the job any longer. I was doing it. This was it.

I got on board my plane and put all my stuff away. I took a deep breath in and then a deep breath out. I set up as much as I could before the passengers started boarding. The flight was from Chicago to Fort Myers, Florida. I had to serve a full dinner service, and I was freaking out at how much I had to set up. I cried in the galley in front of all the other flight attendants, and they were so sweet and helpful. My prep time soon ran out, and I shut all the carts and ovens and started greeting passengers. Once everyone was boarded, we shut the door and taxied off to the runway, getting ready for takeoff. About ten minutes after takeoff, once it was safe to get up and start serving, I had another flight attendant come up and help me a little bit. But after she left and went back to coach, I was in charge of running the show.

First I had to serve the mixed nuts I had preheated. I went to pull the mixed nuts out of the oven, and they were burned to a crisp. To this day, it was the worst I have ever burned anything on an airplane. I couldn't help but laugh. Of course I would burn something my first time in first class. As disappointed as I was in myself, I was full of so much grace. I was learning at a fast rate. I was doing it. I was showing up and doing the best I could. Every day.

———————

There were no red carpets or sparkly moments in those beginning days. There was just a lot of teeth gritting and attitude changing. I had to fight—hard—to find the joy in all my mess-ups and in my mundane. I spent so much of my early twenties trying to control every little thing in life—my relationships, my future, my dreams, my job—thinking I needed to have everything figured out. I wanted to know exactly *how* I was going to get to a place of healthiness and find joy in the midst of everything going on around me, and it drove me nuts to not succeed every day. Failure caused anxiety, depression, stress, and many sleepless nights. But then I'd joyfully discover little pockets of growth that let God's love fill me up and life unfold.

Think about your best days for a moment. The ones where you feel that pit in your stomach soften. Where your mind is at rest, not fighting to hang on to control or overthinking every last detail. Those days when life is just *happening* and you don't have to fight to press the brakes and stay in the present. You are simply present. Where do those best days come from? What do they have in common? If you aren't in that place right now, how can you get there again? Take a minute and list out things you are doing that you are proud of. I bet you can list more than you know. It's probably hard for you, just like it's hard for me.

I am so thankful for my time living with my Vietnamese roommates and learning more about the beauty of Asian culture. I am thankful for all the times I cried at my secret spot and let the Chicago buildings wrap their arms around me. I am overwhelmed in the best way when I think about the burnt airplane nuts, my first days as a flight attendant, and my early twenties. I truly am. I don't regret a single second of it. I do wish I would have loosened my tight grip on trying to control my circumstances though. I want to end this brief glimpse of becoming with that thought.

The world tells us what we should be doing and how we should be succeeding before we even know that it's bossing us around. But simply put, to be doing it—whatever that is for you—is enough. You don't have to punish yourself because you are five steps behind when you think you should be ten ahead. Right where you are—in this very moment in time—is okay. That doesn't mean we get to be complacent or not prioritize growing, but to be here, doing it at all is a reason to celebrate. Loosen your grip on what you think your life is supposed to look like a bit. Trust me. Life is so much more beautiful that way.

Looking back on those early moments, thinking about all I learned, I can clearly see that I was really doing it. I was really living my life. Those days were shaping the way I would grow for a long time to come. All the things I never thought I'd be or do because I never felt good enough or understood enough or loved enough—I've done them. I've been that girl all along. She lived inside of me the whole dang time. Never forget you are doing it—you are living—even if it looks different from how you thought it would.

i met Ben outside of a coffee shop during my first ever trip to California. You could feel his kindness from around the corner, and I just knew he was a kindred spirit. He asked to join me as we both sipped our lattes. I told him I was visiting from Chicago, and he shared with me all of his favorite local spots. We immediately bonded over our love for tattoos. At the time, I had a couple, and he had many. He took me down the long, beautiful road of the stories behind each and every one of his. It was such a special moment to share with a stranger.

He pointed to a specific one on his arm and told me that he got it for his father. Ben and his father bonded deeply over baseball. He told me the words on his arm are a phrase that Hall of Famer Satchel Paige, one of the all-time best pitchers, lived by: "Don't look back, boy." Sitting outside talking to my new friend, hearing why he got those words written on his arm, filled me with a deep feeling of significance. Connecting with other humans is such a beautiful gift.

———

One day, years later, I found myself on the scariest hike of my entire existence. I had just rounded a corner after hiking way too many switchbacks, and I saw the final stretch of the hike out in front of me. Angels Landing was sitting right before my eyes, and I simply could not take in the full beauty of the hike and the scenery in Zion National Park. I also cannot describe how scared I was to hike the remaining portion of the trail.

There was a huge, narrow, never-ending mountain out in front of me that I realized I was going to have to hike up. I saw people holding on to a chain rail moving up the narrow trail, and then I saw different people using the same chain rail to come down the mountain. Yes, a *chain* rail. They were sharing a rusty old chain to pull themselves up and steady themselves down this narrow, skinny, frightening mountain. It was almost as if their hands were doing a little dance, trying to not disturb one another as they shared the same lifeline.

I took a deep breath before I started, not sure if I was going to pass out now or later, and reminded myself how hard I had already worked to get to this point. I had been hiking this trail for hours with my friend Kaitlyn, and this was the grand finale. The other parts of the hike were beautiful, but I knew nothing was going to compare to the view that would be on the other side of this mountain.

I began to pull myself up the mountain, using the

chain rail. Even though it was hard work avoiding people coming down the other side, it ended up being not as bad as I'd anticipated. I could do this. I was going to make it to the end! I could feel it. And then I got to a big peak. I'm talking *big*. At that point, I decided it was a good idea to look back behind me, to see how far I had hiked. Big mistake. I was holding on to the chain for dear life, and then, because I looked backed, I realized what I would be facing on the way back down. I immediately started to freak out. Was a helicopter going to be able to fly out to get me? Was my friend going to have to hike all the way back down to get someone?

What was I going to do? I was so close, but I had no idea how I was going to make it back or even make it to the end of the hike. My anxiety was screaming loud. My hands were shaking from nerves. That's when I remembered Ben and his tattoo: *Don't look back, boy*. I remembered how much courage and motivation his story gave me, and I held tight to that reminder. I could not keep looking back. I had to press forward and remember what was ahead. I pictured the view that was minutes away from me. I stopped looking back, got up, took a deep breath, and looked forward. I pulled myself up with sweaty, shaky hands on the metal chain and prayed that I wouldn't slip and fall off the edge of the mountain. I got low and crawled at some turns because I was terrifed, but I kept moving forward, remembering what was to come.

Not looking down, around, beside me, or behind me—only looking forward.

What felt like an eternity hiking the last few ups, downs, turns, and curves on Angels Landing finally came to a halt. I felt the fresh, clean wind that only comes from being in the center of such pure beauty. It was the most spectacular view I had ever laid eyes on. I could not believe that it was out there in front of me, just waiting to be experienced. I couldn't believe I'd made it that far. Words weren't enough.

———————

Using a literal don't-look-back mountain hiking experience may seem a little corny, but in a moment of true fear, remembering the story of Ben's tattoo really did help me push through. A lot of times when I have been on the cusp of something grand or beautiful in life, I have stopped to look back on the past. New job? It's a dream come true, but then I'll remember how I failed at my old one. New relationship? Well, what if I have the same luck as the last one? I end up spending so much time dwelling on the past that I ruin the excitement of what's to come.

I am constantly realizing that there are many broken, junky things we walk around with daily. Our past, hurt, shame, self-doubt, regret—the list goes on and on. We live in it and sometimes let it fog up our consciousness and hurt our joy. The beauty of everyday, though, is that we get newness. We get fresh love, grace, understanding, and the chance to have at it again. We can take that mindset into experiences as well. We get an unlimited amount of re-do's and restarts and the past doesn't get to have a say. We do.

Sit with me for a second. Are you spending so much time wrapped up in the past that it's stealing room for new, beautiful things in your life to happen? Maybe take some time after this chapter and check yourself. Even though looking back can be a celebratory kind of thing, you can't stay there. Especially if it causes you unhealthiness. Don't look back—unless it's to celebrate, to heal from, to learn from, or to move you forward with loads of joy. Trust what is good and true to push you forward. There is so much beauty that lies ahead.

t hroughout most of my childhood, I had one bright-yellow tooth. Weird, I know. I called it my corn tooth because it looked like I had a piece of corn stuck on my tooth at all times. The doctors said it was either from a fever as a kid or that I fell down and hit it—no one really knew. I finally lost it when I turned eight. The day it fell out, I remember throwing a party with my family because I was so excited it was gone. Funny enough, the tooth that grew in its place came in a little bit crooked. I was supposed to get braces because of it, but I never did. Now it's one of my favorite parts of myself, that crooked tooth.

I can't help but think that stories like this are a theme for this life I get to live. The broken, crooked, messiest, most painful parts about me are the most beautiful. This revelation has shaped the way I see myself and others. It has made me realize that we are all our own kind of beautiful, and it is so special when we let our messy, beautiful selves live. You are actually wonderful, flaws and all. When we speak truth over ourselves like this, we eventually start to believe it.

I feel it's important to shed some light on confidence. As a woman who has walked through a lot in this life, confidence has been a winding, rocky road for me. Not only did I get bullied for most of my childhood because of my tooth, but I also got made fun of a lot for my looks. I was the tall, lanky, overly skinny girl for a very, very long time. Everyone picked on me always. People called me twiggy and a lot of other names—it was hurtful. Being bullied influenced how I presented myself physically and emotionally. I was always outgoing and funny in hopes that people wouldn't find something to pick out that was wrong about me. I never knew how to be my true, authentic self because I hid so many beautiful parts of me for a very long time. I felt like I had to hide the parts of myself that I couldn't help. Our society tells us a lot about who we have to be or not be, doesn't it? I learned young.

On top of being bullied, as I entered my teen years, I learned to find assurance and confidence from the boys I dated. If they said I was pretty, I was pretty. If they liked to do a certain thing, I learned to like that thing as well. I became a blended version of all the people in my life, but not in a good way. I hadn't found my own worth, value, or purpose, so I was swimming all over the place trying to find them. I was letting everyone else decide who I was. It wasn't until I started doing some hard inner work that

I really, truly started to see myself clearly and embrace what made me, *me*.

One of my first realizations was that I didn't like dresses. Dresses gave me big anxiety. I also realized that the color pink was my least favorite color, and floral print just didn't make sense to me. Neither did a lot of makeup or the idea of frying my hair every day in order to feel put together. It's also important to note that this was extremely hard for me later, since becoming a flight attendant involved wearing dresses, high heels, and makeup. I struggled at the beginning of my career to find a balance of what felt like me and what was required of me from my job. Yes, all of these things are very specific to the feminine style, but I realized there were a lot of other things that made me feel like a strong, beautiful woman. I started to focus on what was on the inside of me that could come out to make me feel beautiful. I could be kind to strangers on flights and that looked better than any sort of makeup I wore. I could compliment others and make them feel seen and loved, and that was a much greater feeling than what I felt like when I wore cool outfits or had to put on a dress. As I started to focus on these things, the pressure to be someone I was not became lighter. I started to realize that the things the world tells us to be are so much less important than who we show the world we are. Our true selves are the most beautiful things we can offer up to others.

Please know I'm not saying that owning dresses or wearing pink or loving floral is wrong or weird—these things just didn't make me feel like me. They didn't make me feel like the true Taylor. It took trial and error, but I figured out what made me feel like my true self when I stopped listening to what the world said and paying attention to the actions of everyone else around me.

Now I'm filled with so much love and feel so sure about what I'm called to. It may not look like what everyone else says it should, but *that is okay*. I remind myself of this truth as many times as I need. I get to come home to myself every day. What a gift it is to be me. Beautiful, wonderful me.

I've always felt unconventional. Always the oddball. Always seeing things with a special kind of light because of what I've walked through. But for a really long time, I felt like I was wrong. I felt that it wasn't okay for me not to look or act like everyone else. Like *I* wasn't okay. It's taken a long time, but I'm finally okay just being me. Crusty old Taylor with so much love to give and so much to offer. Sometimes I still have to work to not compare myself to everyone else. Maybe you feel that way too. Just know you aren't alone. You don't have to be like everyone else. You don't have to do what everyone else is doing.

For the longest time I saw myself as the broken girl. I became the things I latched on to in hopes that they would fill me up. All it ended up doing was leaving me even more broken and empty. My pain literally showed on my face. I had the darkest bags under my eyes, and I felt as if I were screaming for help. So when I see photos of myself nowadays, it's really hard for me not to get my heartstrings pulled by the joy that radiates from my face.

I can't believe that God loves me so much he would give me a beautiful comeback story, worth, and this ziplock-bag kind of grace spilled out for everyone to see. I've learned that it's possible to turn your life around. It's possible to dig deep and find that confidence within you. To get out of unhealthy relationships. To stop being unhealthy in relationships. To be passionate about life and what you love. To get up and chase after that thing. To function and grow even while you are messy. To say no. To say yes. To look at yourself and see what is already there. It's possible. I'm a walking testimony with a beating heart that is proof healing can happen. I am all the more beautiful because I am me.

If you are struggling with your confidence or self-worth, let me remind you of this: there is a certain kind of light and beauty that comes with carrying heaviness and persevering. Lean into that. That is beautiful to me. That is beautiful to the world, too, even if they may feel intimidated by it. Try to look at yourself and see what you have become and how far you have come—not what is missing or lacking. There is a fierceness that comes from getting up on your worst days. A special kind of joy that comes from battling on hard days. That stuff just shines out of your face. No matter what you are feeling or what you are holding, take a step back and take a look at yourself. Can you say thank you to where you have come from and to where you are going? Can you see that you are your own kind of beautiful?

You are actually wonderful. When you start looking with eyes that see and believe it, you will find that confidence you are searching for.

One morning I was pouring tomato juice for a passenger on my flight. I was in my own little world, probably talking to myself or singing Justin Bieber in my head, you know, the usual, when I started having a little moment deep down inside.

When I first started out as a flight attendant, I was petrified of tomato juice. Laugh at me all you want, but there was just something about the smell and the texture when I poured it into a glass that I could not get past. I was scared and could not go near it without feeling like I was going to have a full-on freak-out. Probably silly and, yes, a little dramatic, but it was a very real thing a few years ago. If a passenger ever asked me for it, I had to have a moment to pray silently before I stepped near it. I honestly can't tell you when that changed or why I was able to overcome my silly little fear, but I did. I hadn't really thought about it since, but that specific morning I laughed at myself and started thinking about something I had been learning recently: we must celebrate every victory, big or small. We have to take the time to revisit old fears and speak to them from a place of celebration. I can pour tomato juice now. I'm proud.

I can think of a couple of other fears I've kicked in the

behind too. I was scared to death of stingrays, but I swam with them in crystal-clear, blue water. I was petrified to live on my own when my heart was sore and shattered, but I did it anyway. Big victories. Believe it or not, when I first became a flight attendant, I was scared to take that first step to travel internationally, mostly because I was so scared to mess up in a foreign, unfamiliar place. What if I forgot the right charger and my phone died and I got lost? What if I really needed help and didn't speak the correct language? What if I had to drive on the right side of the car when I had only ever driven on the left? So many what-ifs that ended up being silly, and honestly, these are the same what-ifs that make traveling so memorable, as I eventually found out from my own experiences.

As adventurous and outgoing as I am, traveling out of the States was a lot to think about and plan, with all that was going on in my world. I was a newbie flight attendant living in a big city for the first time and was still getting used to the pace of my new life. But I had to remember why I was here in the first place. I was going to spend my whole life traveling. It was time to stop overthinking.

I texted one of my best girlfriends from high school, Bryce, whose mom is a flight attendant as well, and got to scheming with her. Since she had the same travel perks and benefits as I did, we had always talked about being travel buddies and touring the world together. We talked about a lot of places we had a craving to see, but somehow

Paris just felt right for our first trip. Maybe it was the idea of eating chocolate croissants every day or our shared love for Mary-Kate and Ashley Olsen's movie *Passport to Paris*, but eventually the decision was made. We were going to Paris. Next thing I knew, I had packed my bags and was on a plane.

I flew all through the night to get to Paris. I slept about three hours on the flight and had a beautiful, sodium-filled pasta dinner at a time when I should have been sleeping. It was a foggy morning when the plane touched down. I walked off giddy and confused because of the time difference, but I was too excited to care. I was in the City of Love! Bryce and I had to take different flights, as she was coming from Charlotte and I was coming from Chicago, but we met up in the arrivals area. We hugged and talked too fast and could not believe we were finally in Paris. We made a little game plan and looked at Google Maps to figure out how we were going to get to our hostel. (Maybe not your cup of tea, but I always stay in hostels when I travel. Not only does it save you money but you get to meet so many fun new friends from all over the world. I cannot recommend it enough.) Then we headed toward the train that would take us into the city and got scammed.

When I say we got scammed, I mean we got *scammed* within the first thirty minutes of having our feet on solid ground. We were having a lot of trouble figuring out the train ticket machine, and all of a sudden, an old man approached us and asked if we needed help. He told us to put our money in, pushed all the buttons for us, and out popped our tickets. Getting help from locals and making friends—we were already having the best trip ever. We said thank you one too many times and walked toward the ticket scanner to get on the train. However, when we went to scan our tickets, an error message popped up: "Invalid tickets." Bryce and I just looked at each other and tried not to laugh. Of course, we were easy targets. Two loud American girls who had country accents and were having too much fun at a train station. We realized he must have switched our new tickets out with old ones, and we didn't catch it. So we walked back to the ticket kiosk and figured out how to print two tickets on our own. A little victory. We were doing it. Even if it was messy and didn't look like what we thought it was supposed to, we were here and alive. I was kicking my overseas traveling worries in the behind.

We finally arrived at the hostel where we put our bags away and decided to push past our jet lag. We wanted to try to adjust our bodies' internal clocks to the new time zone. Also, who wants to miss a whole day of sunlight when you are in Paris? We surely didn't. We immediately went to the Louvre to see the *Mona Lisa* and all the incredible artwork. To say it was all breathtaking would be an understatement. (The *Mona Lisa* is actually so tiny;

can you believe that?) We took pictures with Mona in a sea full of other humans and spent hours roaming around the museum. There was a marble statue room that was filled with the purest natural light. I can't explain the way it made me feel, but I hugged it and took it all in. Finally, our feet were tired, and the sun was setting. It was time to sleep, and we could not wait. Our first day was a victory. We celebrated with a burger and fries.

Our second day was our first full day in Paris. We decided we wanted to knock out all of the major things first so we could spend the last few days exploring different Paris neighborhoods with no agenda. We woke up early and ate croissants (of course), then headed toward Notre-Dame. When we got off the train at Notre-Dame, that's really when it hit us that we were in Paris. The arches, walls, stained glass, and every last fine detail of Notre-Dame were unlike anything I have ever experienced. Unreal beauty. One of the closest reminders of heaven I have been honored and privileged enough to see. It was incredible being in a place that could make you feel so much peace.

From Notre-Dame, we walked a few steps over to Shakespeare and Company, which is an extremely well-known bookstore. It's an older shop that was born in the 1950s, so it's been around long enough to have that magical, charming, old-bookstore feel, with books stacked floor to ceiling and spilling off every shelf. A book lover's dream. We could have spent the entire day exploring there.

After browsing for as long as we could, we took a long walk along the Seine River, heading toward the Arc de Triomphe and finally, the Eiffel Tower. The child in me was overflowing with joy at the fact that I was going to see the Eiffel Tower in person. As we rounded in and out of Paris's cobblestone streets, we finally turned a corner and saw the tower in all its glory. It was surreal seeing it for the first time. You can spend your whole life hearing about something and seeing pictures of it, but it's nothing compared to actually seeing that thing in real life. The sight of the Eiffel Tower was so unreal that it felt fake; there's no other way to describe the feeling I had. I quickly realized that this is why I had to get out and see the world. This is what it was all about. That feeling of joy and wonder unlike any other.

Finally, the sun crept down, and the Eiffel Tower lit up—and so did my heart. We stayed for a long time, soaking in the beauty all around us. Sitting in the park under the Eiffel Tower and watching it twinkle was something I truly never thought I would do. I'd always dreamed of it, yes, but at the same time, I'd doubted myself to ever get to a place like this.

You know, the things we dream of and ache for can be scary things too. They can feel so far off and hard to reach. I can't tell you how many times I thought of traveling the world but felt like I never would because of my anxiety. Or how I always dreamed of finding my person but thought it was impossible because of the laundry list of mistakes I've made. Have you ever felt this way? That the things you want or dream about the most just seem absolutely, downright scary or impossible to get to? How can good, beautiful things be scary things too? This trip taught me that I could show up scared to do something I really wanted to do. Even if I'm there with a fearful heart and shaky hands. We can celebrate beautiful things and small things and big things. We can celebrate the hard stuff too. Most of the time, it all leads to more growth, more courage, and a lot more love.

My last day in Paris was probably my favorite day out of them all. My flight attendant friend from Chicago joined us for the day, and we picnicked under the Eiffel Tower and ran all over town. We danced and we laughed and we lived fully. It was a breath of fresh air. Bryce and I had decided that since we had one more person with us, we were going to splurge and get a private apartment to stay in for our last night. I had booked it months in advance, so everything was all set up. All we had to do was check out of our hostel, take the train, and check in at the apartment. I messaged our host before we hopped on the train to head over. She didn't answer my messages, and I started to get a little worried but shrugged it off, figuring everything would work out and we could just knock on the door once we arrived.

It did not work out like that. As we walked off the train with our backpacks and luggage and turned the corner to our final destination, we realized it was a huge apartment complex. There was a massive door that led into a courtyard, but in order to even get inside, we needed a code. That's when I started to panic. I didn't have international cell service, so I couldn't just get on my phone to text or call her. This was going to be some sort of adventure.

We quickly found a nearby café that had Wi-Fi, and I tried again to get in touch with our host. As we were sitting there, I realized I didn't even know how to enter a Parisian number into my phone properly. We all laughed at our own cluelessness. I know handling such a stressful situation with laughter seems far-fetched, and I know that this is probably the only time I have ever handled such a big traveling mistake with so much grace, but I think that I was in so much shock after the chaos that all I had left in me was laughter. I also was with Bryce, who was such a dear friend and positive human, and I knew that we would be okay. The people you surround yourself with truly do make life's hardest moments much more bearable.

We started scanning the café to see if anyone looked like they might be able to help us. We asked a few people for help, and they didn't really understand what we were saying. The language barrier is real, and sadly we didn't speak any French. Just as we were about to give up hope, a younger man around our age sat down near us, and we saw an opportunity. We started talking to him, and he was so sweet and tried to help us as best as he could. We were using Google Translate and showing him what was wrong. He started typing numbers into his phone and making calls. We finally figured out how to enter our rental host's number properly, and we sent her a message and waited. We passed the time by getting to know our hero who saved the day. He told us about life in Paris, growing up there, and how much he loved it. We loved hearing how it had shaped him, and we kept talking until he had to leave and we said our thank-yous one more time. His kindness to three strangers in a café is something I will never forget.

We still hadn't heard from our host, so we decided to wait out in front of the building for someone to come out. We could sneak in without the front gate code, then knock on the front door of our host's apartment and wait. After waiting out front for what seemed like forever, we finally got in! We headed up to her apartment and knocked, and guess what? Not a peep from the other side. We really couldn't figure out what was going on. Why would she not answer us, and why would she not be home to let us in? It was almost three hours after check-in time.

We headed down to the courtyard in the building to figure out what we needed to do. As we were all sitting there talking, I decided to pull up the booking confirmation to see if I was missing something. Was there a lockbox with a key we were missing? Were we here too early? What was going on? As I scrolled through the confirmation, all of a sudden something caught my eye. Before I had time to process what I was reading, I started to laugh. The girls looked at me and said, "Taylor, *what?*"

I realized that I had booked the apartment for the right days but the wrong year. I'd booked it for next year. *The next year!* Who does something like that? I could not believe it. I was crying but also laughing at the same time. My friends were really understanding, and they laughed a lot too. What a story. Bryce said I was officially banned from ever booking anything when traveling with her again. But because of our mishap, we ended up meeting some really beautiful people. I survived my first big traveling mistake, and I was better because of it. I was going to celebrate that.

By God's sweet grace, the previous place we'd stayed at had open rooms again. So the anxiety of having nowhere to stay for our last night was lifted immediately. We headed back to our old hostel and continued laughing over bread and wine that night. I truly thought we had wasted hours that day waiting around, but in the end I realized the mishap had taught me how to celebrate every victory.

My trip to Paris taught me to embrace the beauty that life so freely gives to us. Traveling, I was realizing, was a healing thing for me. It forever screams beauty, and it pushes you to chase down joy. To be the best version of yourself. From strangers and their stories to all the nooks and crannies of a new place to explore, there is so much to celebrate. I think a lot of times we imagine victories have to be big or monumental—the things we can't wait to share on social media to get us that validation. Those moments are important, and we should celebrate the big milestones. But I want you to see that victories don't always have to be these big, glamorous things. Victories can be the stuff we overcome and grow from, like traveling for the first time or pouring tomato juice.

What comes to mind when you think about something worth celebrating in your life? Did you slip up on your trip of a lifetime and laugh about it too? Did you take the wrong turn and find somewhere even better? Did you finally figure out how to parallel park properly? That stuff is worth celebrating. When we start to pay attention and celebrate the things we don't think matter, we open our eyes to the magic of small moments. Gratitude for the small stuff is a muscle most of us don't work out enough, but it's there, and it is so good. Let's start to celebrate our screw-ups and mess-ups and our big and small victories.

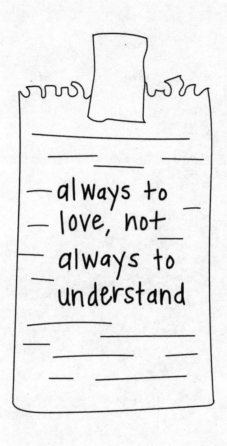

m y story is one that comes with a lot of heaviness for me. It's hard sharing parts of growing up that have shaped the person I have become, while at the same time trying to protect those humans who are a part of my story. I'm going to do the best I can.

I was born in Greensboro, North Carolina, late one April night. I didn't come too early or too late; I was right on time. I spent my early years living there until I was almost two, and then we moved to Florida where my sister was born. My parents divorced a few years later. I was too young to understand why or how. It's really hard to explain those things to a five-year-old. I realize how hard it must have been for my family to try to explain the real, raw, messy things that come from love and relationships. After my parents split, I remember carrying around a heavy, confused feeling because so much didn't make sense. The weight of the world felt like my only friend. So much of my childhood felt misunderstood and hidden. I always felt like I had to fix everything and that I had to keep a tight grip on things so I could control the outcome.

I would get so upset when things didn't work out because so much of my life already felt broken and stale. I can now pinpoint that these were my first days struggling with anxiety and depression.

When my parents first split, they had joint custody. My sister and I would spend one week at Mom's and then one week at Dad's. Even though we spent some time in therapy to help us kids handle the divorce, neither one of my parents really explained to us what was happening. These moments of feeling confused and without love led me to believe I had to keep everything hidden, since so much was hidden from me. Eventually my dad found his person, Amy, who became my stepmother. At the same time, my biological mom fell off the deep end. She got into big trouble with alcohol, addiction, and unhealthy relationships. From there, our relationship started spiraling. She promised me the world, all while never showing up. We still saw her occasionally, but the memories I have of that time hurt me to this day. I can sometimes still taste that specific feeling of loneliness I carried as a kid.

My biological mother also ended up getting remarried, and I received a few new siblings, but I try to block these years out of my memory as best as I can. My father, stepmother, sister, and new baby brother were my family. We eventually left Florida and moved back to North Carolina, where we welcomed my baby sister into the world. At this point, my mother and I had a falling out.

She had rarely been there for me in my early years, and even the occasional times when she was there, our relationship was full of pain.

One year passed without talking to my biological mother, then two, and then before I knew it, over ten years had gone by. My dad worked sunup to sundown, and my stepmom was raising the four of us—it was a lot. I didn't really know how to process my complicated family dynamics as a teenager; I just tried to stay as busy as I could. I left the house at nineteen, and I was so ready to live on my own and create my own home. I needed to create an environment where I felt free and loved. I knew my parents loved me; I just think the absence of the two most important people in my life—with my dad working long hours and my biological mom working through her own problems—really got to me. It wasn't until years later that I finally opened up about those experiences and began to process everything as an adult.

———

I got the call on an overcast Tuesday right after I landed in Miami. I had been away from home for four years and was currently living in Chicago, while my family recently had moved and was calling Texas home. Do you know that feeling of anxiety you get when you see you are getting a call from someone who doesn't usually call you, and you immediately start to freak out? That's the feeling that rose in my chest when I looked down at my ringing phone. I saw my stepmother's name and knew something was wrong. I frantically answered the call while walking from a completed flight to my next one, and all I could hear on the other end was yelling and noise. I stayed on the phone for a second, trying to get someone to talk, but I couldn't figure out what was going on. In the end, I hung up the call and texted, *Is everything okay?* It took a few hours before I heard anything back, but when I finally did get in touch with my stepmom, she was hysterical.

I couldn't seem to put the pieces together, but I got enough information to understand that a close family friend in Texas, Parker, was going through a mental breakdown. My stepmom was devastated and had no idea what to do. I didn't either. There was talk of police and a mental hospital, and I just couldn't bear it. Parker had to be okay. He just had to.

Eventually Parker was sent to a hospital and spent some time away from home getting help. It was really hard for me because I lived thousands of miles away, and with my crazy work schedule, I couldn't get there quickly. Even if I could have gotten there easily, what would I have said? What could I do?

I know the struggle with mental health because it's one that is real in my life every day. I know how hard it is. But this was something for me to carry, not Parker, not someone I loved. What is there to do when the ones we love aren't okay? How was I supposed to continue on with everyday life when I could get a call at any minute that Parker was not with us anymore? The heaviness that comes with questions like these felt unbearable and overwhelming.

Time passed, and my friend is still on a mental health journey. They've gotten a diagnosis and are working toward a healthier life every day. I finally got the chance to fly to Texas for a quick visit, where I saw that they were doing the best that they could. I cried a lot of heavy tears and asked *why* over and over again. I held on to my friend for dear life because I couldn't imagine a world without them in it.

While in town visiting Parker, I sat outside on one hot, Texas night on my family's back porch. As I sat with my grandmother, Mimi, and my stepmom, catching up and talking through my friend's journey, Mimi looked over at me and said, "Taylor, we always have to love, we do not always have to understand." I don't know why, but at that moment, hearing those words brought instant healing. Those few words bunched together felt like a gentle hand being placed over years of hurt. The truth in them was so profound it took me back to parts of myself that were still clenched up and holding on for dear life. *Always to love, not always to understand.*

I thought about how much God loves me and how much he loves you. I thought about how he accepts us just as we are. I thought about the countless people whose actions or broken parts I don't fully comprehend. Heck, I barely understand my own. I thought about my biological mother who chose addiction over loving her daughter. I thought about how she missed out on a relationship with me—a truth that breaks me daily. I thought about all of the people I'm called to love, even if I don't understand them. Didn't Jesus say love was the most important commandment of them all? To love him? To love our neighbors? It's so much easier when we understand them, isn't it?

It's been a constant struggle: letting go of the grip I have on trying to understand people and hard situations and choosing to straight-up love them anyway. I've been hurt by people deeply, just like I've done so to others. I know you can relate. Relationships require a constant wave of grace and forgiveness. Always coming back, over and over, no matter how many times it takes. In moments when I get anxious, am hurt, or feel deeply confused at how things work out and happen, I remind myself of Mimi's words. I'm here to love. I don't have to be consumed with understanding.

Think about all the people in your life who have caused you pain. Whether their actions came from their own brokenness, mental health struggles, or unhealthiness, the reason people cause us pain is hard to understand. When have you tried to understand someone before loving them? Who comes to mind for you? We spend a lot of time trying to wrap our brains around the why or the how in order to understand people. Don't get me wrong, it's helpful for about five minutes. Then you know what it leads to? Anxiety, stress, bitterness, and—most of the time—more pain. It's so much better to love than to try to understand. I also think it's important to note that loving people doesn't mean that it looks like a Nicholas Sparks book or that you are best friends with them. Loving people can mean boundaries and distance. Loving people can be honesty. Loving people looks like a whole heck of a lot of things.

I've had to learn to love people where they are and not where I want them to be. I've had to set down my needs and the yearning inside to understand everything that happens or why people are the way they are. I've taken time to make that love muscle stronger than my need to understand.

———

I sadly haven't had that big, healing, forgiving conversation with my biological mother yet. There have been a couple of Facebook messages and one phone call I placed over the course of almost fifteen years. Does it make me sad? Absolutely. Have I forgiven her on my own time? Indeed. Do I love her? Yes. Do I understand her? No. The same goes for my friend. I still don't understand their struggle and pain. Their broken parts hurt, not because I am disappointed in them but because I don't understand and can't help. Yet I remember Mimi's words loud and clear when I struggle: *Always to love, not always to understand.* I hope that you can remember them as well.

Jesus calls us to a special kind of life. A life paved with love, grace, and acceptance over understanding. Adhering to these principles is one of the hardest things about choosing a life with him. I can promise that when you do, things get a lot lighter. We just have to stick with Love.

i share often about the everyday magic of kindness, and I know that may sound a little strange. The everyday magic of kindness doesn't always mean buying coffee for the person behind you in the drive-through, complimenting a stranger, or hanging a little piece of paper with kind words up on an airplane window. It's this special nook of faith that I feel like I have stumbled on. I cherish it so much, and kindness is the best and easiest way that I access Love on a daily basis. Do you know one of the most beautiful ways you can access this everyday magic of kindness too? By seeing the good in people. Let me show you what I mean by sharing a few of my favorite passenger stories.

Working as a flight attendant, my favorite kind of trip to fly is a three-day trip. If I am going to pack up all of my stuff, do my hair and get into uniform, and drag my three pieces of luggage up the stairs to the train and to the airport, you bet it's going to be worth it. To me, only being gone a day is not worth all of that hard work, so I would rather just be gone for three days. That means I spend two nights in different cities.

During one specific trip, I was just about to finish up my last flight of three days, heading home to Chicago. I was so excited to get into my bed, read Harry Potter, and eat ice cream. On that last flight to Chicago, I noticed the cutest, sweetest family sitting near me as I was setting up the carts for service. Their three girls were the cutest little humans and had blonde hair so light that it looked white. They stuck out to me immediately. I could feel it in my gut that they were good people, and usually that feeling is right.

As we were shuffling to collect all of our belongings out of the overhead bins, about to run off the airplane, head home, and go our separate ways, I ran into the cute family I had noticed during the flight. Or, rather, the girls ran over to me in the terminal, smiling. This sweet family and I started talking, and we walked out of the airport together. I learned that they had been traveling all day so they could visit their grandparents in the States for the holidays. One of the little ones was telling me that they were missionaries in China. I asked her what kind of mission work she did, and she looked at me with wide eyes and the toothiest grin and said, "I love Jesus; that's what kind of mission work I do!" She was so full of light. So excited to say that. So proud.

I said, "Well, that's amazing! You want to know a secret? I love Jesus too!"

Her jaw dropped. She had a little twinkle in her eye.

She was practically yelling as she responded, "Really?!" She was excited to have a friend who loved the same guy she did. She then told me I would probably see her again in a few weeks because I would be working on her flight back to China. She was dictating my schedule now. I couldn't help but laugh.

Kids are my favorite for this reason. Always so innocent telling us exactly what they think with absolutely no filter. Filled with so much wonder and whimsy. I told her I wished I was working on her China flight because that would be awesome, but some other nice flight attendants would be working it instead. She got a little upset and looked at her sisters, then something clicked for her. She started glowing. I will never forget her next words to me. "Well, if I don't see you again here on earth, that's okay because I'll get to see you up in heaven!" My heart. My stinking heart. I've never had a stranger get so excited to hear about my faith. She was seven years old. This moment has stuck with me for a very, very long time.

I think God blessed me with a beautifully strong sense of intuition. A lot of times I can just talk to people or make eye contact with them and feel what they are going through. Maybe it's because pain has been such a close friend of mine that I can see it in other people as well.

One day at work, a woman walked onboard my early morning flight with a swollen face and her sunglasses on. I thought, *Wow, she looks really sad*. I could just feel it in her presence. As boarding ended and I got a chance to look around, I noticed that the seat next to her was empty, and I listened to a gut feeling. As our plane was about to take off, she removed her glasses, and I finally got a peek at those raccoon eyes she had from crying. It's a face I knew all too well from my own heartache. I was also in the middle of losing love again, and I think that's why I was so in tune with her sadness. It's always been this way, but on that specific day, I just knew we needed each other.

I got through with my drink service and headed toward her seat. I got down to her level, crouching in the aisle so I could feel connected with her. I started with a little small talk and found out her name was Sarah, even though I already knew that from my paperwork. We talked about the weather, where she was traveling to and from, if she needed anything, and all of the other little things you talk about on a plane.

Eventually I told her that she was beautiful and loved. Her tears really came then. She grabbed my hand and shared with me that the flight she was on was supposed to be her and her husband's anniversary trip. The night before the trip, however, he'd left her and filed for divorce. She was heartbroken. You could see it on her face and feel it in her hands. She told me she was going on vacation anyway to learn about herself and how to be brave. I knew those feelings all too well. Do you know what I got to do for the rest of the flight? I got to hold her hand and let her cry on my shoulder. I got to share some of my stories and speak life over her. I got to have that moment with her, and it was so special.

I was working first class, which, if you don't know by now, is not my favorite place to be. It was a quick flight to a smaller Texas town, and all of my passengers were so kind. I took a walk through the cabin to make sure everyone was doing okay, and that's when I really, truly saw how precious the couple sitting in 3A and 3B were. They must have been over eighty years old, and they wouldn't let go of each other's hands. I was sobbing at this point because old couples have the most special place in my heart. I think I could write a whole chapter on them. I had to look away because if I kept staring, my tears would have made a scene.

I went into the galley to take a second and fidget with something when all of a sudden, I heard a weird but oddly familiar noise. It wasn't an alarming noise, but I couldn't figure out what had caused it. I started to check around my area. *Weird*, I thought. Then I peeped my head out into the airplane aisle, and that's when I saw it. The older man in 3B was taking film photos on his windup camera of his wife sitting at the window. Oh, you thought I was sobbing before? Well, now I was a complete puddle. I walked over to them and let them know how absolutely precious I thought they were. They blushed and told me that their grandson had bought them first-class tickets, and this was their first time flying up front. They wanted to remember this moment. It was one of the purest, sweetest moments I've had to this day. I took a mental picture of the couple and held on to it long after we'd said our goodbyes. Seeing the good in people is how we see God all around us. We love people more deeply when we see them as being more like him.

Seeing that magic, that everyday kindness I speak so highly of, is something you and I have to choose to do every single day. We have to choose to love others and to see the good in them. On our bad days and great days. I really, truly, wholeheartedly believe that in order to be kind to others as a daily act of love, we have to see the good in them—even if we have to dig deep to see it. You can be kind for a minute or for five seconds easily, but what about when someone is rude to you or aggravates you with their demand for a Diet Coke in a can when there is none left? Really, sometimes the last thing I want to do is be kind.

Keeping these special moments close and practicing that art of seeing the good in people has been vital for me. So I want to invite you in on this choice. Maybe you are in a customer-service job like me, or maybe you are simply a person working on how you treat others around you. We live in a painful world where people can be so ugly; kindness these days seems like a workout that no one wants to warm up for. What if we really, really dug deep and pushed hard to see the good in people? What if we had memories of precious, special moments in our back pockets to use whenever being kind got really hard? We are all trying to make it. We are learning how to heal from heartbreak. How to manage death, debt, or depression. How to be in love. How to do Whole30 and not cheat on day three. All of it. We are all works in progress. A musician I admire, Sleeping at Last, has a line in his song "Saturn" that goes, "How rare and beautiful it is to even exist." Think about that for a minute. You and I are alive here, breathing, living, and loving—that is a miracle in itself. Remember to keep digging and pushing hard to see the good in people. I promise it will open your eyes to the magic I am talking about.

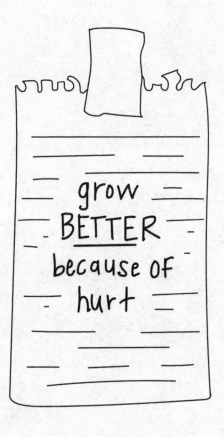

h ave you ever gotten off of a really long plane ride and, within thirty minutes of having your feet on solid ground, found yourself swimming with sea turtles? My answer changed when I landed in Hawaii in 2015. Yes, I actually said sea turtles, and I really mean it. Real-life, hundred-pound sea turtles in all of their glory. Swimming alongside them was so beautiful that my tears clogged up my goggles, and the people on the beach probably heard me screaming with disbelief through my snorkel. I simply could not believe it.

I had a friend named Erika who was working on Hawaii's Big Island. Erika had said that I could come visit whenever I felt like it, and goodness did I ever feel like it. A few months prior to this trip, I had called off my wedding, and I was still healing from being in that unhealthy relationship. I tend to do this thing where I run away to some exotic place when the weight of the world feels too much. And this was definitely one of those times—it was the week of the wedding that had been called off. So I decided to spend what I thought would be one of the hardest weeks of my life in Hawaii, soaking up as much beauty as I could. Our pain makes us really appreciate the beauty when we look for it, doesn't it?

My sweet friend picked me up, and we headed straight to a beautiful beach surrounded by volcanic rock to meet up with some of Erika's friends. That's where I got to meet the turtles and swim in crystal-clear water. The next days were filled with a lot of smoothie bowls, sunshine, and raw, honest conversations about how broken and scared I was. How stretching it felt being there celebrating so much beauty even though my heart was aching. I remember lying in bed, staring at the ceiling the night before what was supposed to be my wedding day. I still can feel that heaviness when I close my eyes. I remember digging so deep to feel like everything would be okay. I sat up in bed for a long time talking to God, repeatedly asking him to keep me close to peace and make me feel okay. I think this is the most beautiful way we can show up to our pain: just as we are. Most of the time we are given exactly what we need; we just don't always see it that way until later on.

I woke up the next morning, the morning of my supposed-to-be wedding day, and took some deep breaths. Erika had a surprise adventure to keep me as upright and okay as I could be. I put on my adventure clothes, packed up, and we set out to Hilo, which was about two hours away from where we were in Kona. We found out we took the really, *really* long way there, but that was just fine; we didn't mind. Hilo and the winding roads we drove down were bursting with beauty. A suspicious amount of beauty; I could barely take it all in. We drove past volcanic rock, up mountainsides, through fog, over waterfalls, and by palm trees—all while the windows were down and God hugged us through the sunshine. Our first stop was Rainbow Falls. It has an incredible view of a waterfall and the perfect banyan tree to climb. It made the five-year-old inside my heart go absolutely crazy.

After a few pit stops to see the beauty just hanging around waiting to be felt, we headed to our main destination, the spot Erika knew I needed to see. We pulled up and parked a little bit away, but as soon as I walked down the grassy path to the hidden spot, my heart started skipping beats. As I walked closer and understood what my eyes were seeing, I realized I was standing in front of a massive, shady tree growing over a huge, deep swimming hole. The tree's roots were gigantic, and on each and every one of them, I saw a different young boy staring back at me. Most were laughing and playing, and some were doing backflips off of high branches and into the water. Something about that scene felt like a gift I didn't know I needed. I needed this. The inner child in me needed this.

I realized those brave boys were swinging from the vines and jumping from the highest point off of the tree and into the hole. The jump must have been at least twenty feet! I was standing there trying to do the math in my head when I got this warm feeling in my gut telling me, *You are going to do this.* I had to do it; I had to jump off of the top of this tree.

I decided to start small and grabbed on to a little rope swing. I hit the freezing water and stayed under for a second, letting the cold water soak into my sore places. I laughed as I jumped over and over again; I couldn't contain my joy. As I unsteadily worked my way up to the highest spot in the tree, all the boys became my cheerleaders. I was wobbly from nerves, and they kept chanting me on. I finally climbed my way to the top, and I looked down and let go without a care in the world.

These are the moments I will hold on to. The ones where I stood up and chose to get out and live because of the hurt. The day I was supposed to get married ended up being one of my favorite days of my life, in a way I never could have predicted. Every part of my aching body wanted to lie in bed and hide away from the world. That's how pain makes us feel a lot of times. It's so much easier to binge a show on Netflix and hide away from life than it is to get up, put pants on, and simply live.

When my future kids ask me to tell them a bedtime story about an adventure, this will be the first one that spills out of my heart. Hawaii taught me that when I choose to reach out and stretch deep and wide—even when I am hurting and broken—so much growth comes because of it. There is so much beauty waiting to be spilled out over every crack and corner of our broken parts. We just have to find the courage to get up and let it happen. That's the hardest part.

There are many—too many—moments in my life where I can still feel an ache. Hurt pierces deep sometimes, doesn't it? It can feel unbearable and almost like a shadow we can't run away from. If you are reading this right now and feel a heaviness deep inside you, whatever it may be from, I double-dog dare you to get up and go outside. Go on a walk. Put your phone down and look up. I dare you to grab your keys and drive with no Google Maps. Roll down the windows if you can and just breathe that air in. You are alive and you are doing it—even if it's hard or hurtful as growing can be sometimes. Growth doesn't always look the same every time. Love meets us where we are. Just like it met me at that secret, magical swimming hole in Hawaii.

Calling off a day that I had dreamed about for much of my life was one of the most difficult decisions I have ever been a part of. But you know what? Looking back on it now, it was the best decision that could have ever happened to me.

So what I want to know is, what are you thinking of right now? When you picture me hanging from the top of a twenty-foot tree about to pee my pants and jump, what was that moment for you? Where do you picture yourself? What are you doing? If you haven't jumped yet or had that moment to heal and grow, how can we get you there? How can we grow so the pain doesn't become our boss? It's not easy. Not every day looks like Hawaii and secret swimming holes and glittery things. It's real, raw, honest work to choose to get up on our hardest days. It's honestly an everyday kind of work, and it is dang hard work. I realized (thank you, therapy) that I like to hold on to my hurt on purpose, as twisted as that may sound. Is that something you do too? My therapist has used the words "playing the victim" one too many times before, and every time she does, I look around for the nearest exit I can bolt out of. It can be comforting at times. Our hurt is the best kind of cheerleader to stay angry and stagnant. Pain is such a good liar and gives us control. When we hold on to it, we don't have to heal, but choosing to become like Love requires us to let go, mostly of our own control. That is something I am still learning how to do.

Growing better because of our hurt is a daily choice. I show up most days with shaky hands. I don't always let go every time. But guess what? I show up the next day, and I am becoming better because of it. I hope you join in on it too. Whether you have started the process already or whether it's your first time realizing you need to let go of some hurt, write it down, yell it out, or jump off of a tree into a swimming hole in Hawaii if that is something you can make happen. It's time. And growth will come.

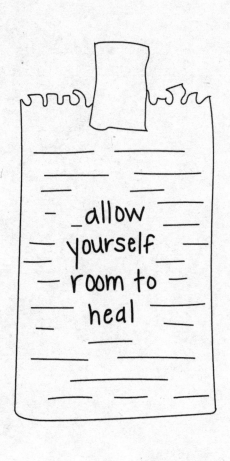

i n the summer of 2015, I had a lot of big life decisions to make. They were ones that I would rather run from at all costs, but it was time to make changes. Even though I'd recently moved from Chicago to Washington, DC, I realized after about six months that I just didn't want to be there anymore. I'd moved there mostly based on a future I was planning with someone that ended up not working out. You know, that wedding that was called off. Washington, DC, wasn't really a good fit for me either.

I came to a crossroads one day trying to figure out the next step forward in my life. Should I stay in DC to see what could happen, or should I move somewhere else? After a lot of wrestling, I decided I wanted to move back to Chicago. I felt like I hadn't really given life there my best shot. I had just started to make friends before I left, finding my favorite coffee shops and local spots and really getting to know the city. It was time to go back and give it my all. No more moving for the wrong relationships.

One weekend, when I had a few days off from flying, I went back to Chicago to look at apartments. Most of them were two bedrooms because I planned on finding a roommate, but the more I looked, the more I felt this nudge in my heart. I kept feeling like I needed to live alone, and, let me tell you, that made my extroverted self so uncomfortable. Living alone when I was healing from losing an unhealthy relationship and walking away from my dream of getting married was the *last* thing I wanted to do. Still, that feeling persisted, and I figured there must be a deeper reason as to why. Maybe I was supposed to do something uncomfortable that would grow me in a way I couldn't even recognize I needed. So I decided to view a studio apartment. As soon as I walked in, I knew it was mine. It was 450 square feet of healing and love. I could feel it. I signed the lease papers that same day. I was moving back to Chicago.

I packed my belongings in DC into three suitcases and moved all my things via an airplane. With my skateboard under my arm and too many bags to manage, I hopped on the Chicago Blue Line train and headed to pick up the keys to my new studio apartment in the heart of Logan Square. My suitcases were full of books, a few favorite mugs, and some clothes. I got a twin-size bed that fit snugly into a nook that was supposed to be the closet. It wasn't perfect, but it was mine. I was taking care of myself, and I was going to have a safe place to heal and grow.

Every summer of my childhood, my family packed up the car, hit the road, and spent the whole summer on Lake Winona in Warsaw, Indiana, at my grandparents' lake house. One day after I'd moved back to Chicago, I heard there was talk of selling the lake house, and I knew I had to make it out there just in case it was the last time. A few weeks later, I flew from Chicago to Indiana to meet my family and spend the week at the lake house. It was nostalgic and magical, and I won't ever forget saying goodbye to such a special place that held so many memories for us. Once my week at the lake house was almost over, my parents decided that they would drive me back home to my apartment in Chicago and take me to IKEA on the way into the city. I usually feel bad when people offer to buy me things, but this trip was special. My heart was sore, my parents loved me, and I needed all the help I could get. I just didn't know how to ask for it.

They ended up buying me two chairs, an AC unit, some kitchen appliances, bed stuff, and all sorts of little things you need when you start from scratch. My parents spent the day with me, and on their way out of the city, they took me to get a bike. I remember them dropping me off at a gas station so we could go our separate ways. I got out of the minivan and onto my bike, and I'll never forget saying goodbye to them. They both looked me in the eye and asked, "Are you sure you are going to be okay?"

The truth was, I had no idea. I just knew I didn't have

to have it all figured out. I just had to keep stepping forward, one foot in front of the other.

On that first night alone, sitting in one of my new chairs, I pulled out a bag of grapes and tried to figure out what to do with myself. I was broken, mad at Jesus, and starting over, again, in a city where I barely knew anyone. The only thing I could think to do was try to get my mind off of my life. So I decided to read. In between taking breaks to cry, I started and finished *The Little Prince*. I love that book so much. When I closed the book, I looked at my empty grape bowl. I was alone with myself and my brokenness. And I was scared. Really, *really* scared. I had been uncomfortable with being alone for so long. I clung to relationships and unhealthy love so I didn't have to dig deep and look at my mess. I was scared I was never going to be okay. I was scared to be alone with my thoughts and my sadness. Living alone brought everything out in the open, and there was no running away or hiding from it all. I had to face it.

Summer came and went, and even though I had moved back to Chicago, I was still starting and ending my flight attendant trips out of DC. I slept at the airport in DC and came home to my studio in Chicago on my days off. I wanted to be done with DC, but my transfer to be based in Chicago wasn't going through, and I was waiting and trying to be patient. (Spoiler alert: it ended up taking nine months for my transfer to go through.) Winter was coming, and I was not ready. Not only was I extremely depressed, but I was scared of spending the winter alone.

On my days off, I biked to new coffee shops in Chicago and pretended to be busy just to keep myself distracted. One day I picked up the first Harry Potter book, and I finally found something to keep me busy. I made some new best friends at Hogwarts: Harry, Hermione, and Ron. Over the next six months, I read every single book while lying in bed eating Neapolitan ice cream. It was my thing, and that's how I remember this season. My broken heart and my healing self were cooped up in my studio apartment, eating ice cream and reading Harry Potter.

————————

Allowing, and giving, myself room to heal. That's what this season was for me: living alone and forcing myself into something immensely scary. I knew I wouldn't be able to run from myself. There wasn't another option. I knew if I was going to find the girl I wanted to become, I had to fight to find her. Some days I came home and immediately crashed to the kitchen floor because I couldn't make it to my bed. Some days I opened up the blinds and let the light in, but other days I kept them closed.

Maybe you don't know what it's like to have to sit on the shower floor because your heart feels too weak to stand, but maybe you know exactly what it's like. And if you do, I'm here to tell you: it gets better.

It gets so much better. I can truly, wholeheartedly say that and mean it. I am living a life that looks completely different from everything I had planned, but I've tasted healing. I lived on my own in the cutest little studio apartment. There were days when I opened my door and felt safe, and there were days when I opened my door and it felt as heavy as a rock. But by taking the time and making that room to heal, I finally started to see the fruit that came from doing the inner work to heal. Slowly but surely, my heart felt like beating. It felt like being alive and not sore.

I know some of you reading this are crying with me because you get it. You know how hard losing love is. You know how hard it is to be completely alone while everyone else in the entire universe is finding love—or at least that's what it feels like. You know how hard and painful it is to grow by being torn down. But sometimes we have to do that. We have to be completely stripped, and we have to face isolation head-on. I've been learning that growth isn't always running through a field of beautiful flowers. Sometimes growth is digging up bad roots and replacing bad soil so that more beautiful, wonderful things have room to grow. Being cut down hurts, but the next season that is waiting for you is worth it. Every tear shed, every painful wound found on your heart, is worth it.

The fact that I haven't pulled out all of my hair yet is a miracle to me. The fact that I got out of bed today and smiled at a stranger is probably the biggest accomplishment of my day. I don't have instructions for how to keep fighting for joy when it's the last thing you want to do. All I can tell you is that you have to do it. When you open your heart, even just a tiny bit, the light will find a way in. You have to be willing. You have to keep fighting for yourself. You have to create that safe space so you can allow yourself room to heal. You must decide to commit to the inner work.

I wish I had big, fancy, bright words. I wish I could tell you everything is going to be all right, but you know what? Sometimes everything really isn't all right. The beautiful thing is that you can admit that. You can admit you're not okay. You can admit that life is horrible and downright evil sometimes; but once you do, don't stay there. Make the decision, as many times as it takes, to look pain straight in the eye. Swallow spoonfuls of courage and fight. It took me almost six months of grieving alone in my studio apartment, but one day after I cried as many tears as I could cry, I got up and decided not to stay where I was anymore. I got up and opened my eyes to the hope, joy, and love all around me. I found it in city skylines, in my passengers on airplanes, in sunrises and sunsets, in black cups of coffee, in jumping on hotel beds, and in strangers' laughter. I found it everywhere. And that's exactly what you can do too.

Whatever personal healing you need to experience, get to a place where you can do that. Take it all in, day by day. Start opening up to others—healthy people who are able to love you and speak life into you are the people you need. Stick with those guys; they are vital to your growth. If something is wrong, air it out. Don't hold it in and let it overtake you. Vulnerability is a beautiful thing. It's a gift, and God gave us a voice for a reason. We were given a voice so we could let others in. Give your heart that space and time to feel safe or to feel anything at all. Through the searching, the tears, the breakdowns, the heaviness, and the rebuilding, you'll find healing. Trust me with this one.

h ave you ever heard of the Enneagram? It's this beautiful personality framework that helps you learn more about yourself and how you are wired. It contains nine numbers, starting at one, which represent nine different beautiful and unique personality types. I took the test and found out I was a Seven. The enthusiast. As I read through my type's character qualities and traits, I started looking around, freaking out, trying to figure out who was stalking me. It was so on point. I felt understood and seen, but I also wanted to crawl into a hole because it listed out the Seven's unhealthy qualities too. Sevens are known for being extremely passionate and overly excited about everything. We want to do everything. We want to see everything. We have a million hobbies because we just get so excited about everything. I mean *everything*. Everything is my favorite y'all. It's a blessing and a curse.

As I kept reading about who I am and how I am wired, I started getting discouraged. Even though I feel so much passion for all of my projects and hobbies, I can get overwhelmed and spread myself too thin sometimes. I start a lot of beautiful things, all with good intentions, but have a hard time following through. I get extremely overwhelmed. A lot of times I stop doing things and put my dreams on hold.

When I think about the list of dreams and passions that I so desperately want to live out, I'm ashamed that I don't always have the discipline to follow through. I want to grow healthier in this messy area of my life. I want to make my wildest dreams come to life, not just halfway start them and move on to the next best idea. But when I start to get down on myself about this, I remember that there have been times where I have followed through and pushed hard to finish something I started. Some of my favorite projects have been born from digging deep and finishing, even when it was the last thing I wanted to do.

There was an anonymous quote that I stumbled on years ago while scrolling through Tumblr, and it really changed and shaped the heartbeat of my life: "If I am not encouraging and inspiring others, what am I doing?" When I first read those words, they shook me. I didn't know how to gather up all the things that made me, *me* and unfold them into something that was bigger than myself. Something that encouraged and inspired others like that quote challenged me to do.

One day I sat down with a friend, trying to figure out how to take my ball of dreams, passions, and knots out of my head and into the big, beautiful world where they needed to be. She spent a lot of time listening to me ramble on about how I knew I was called to love the heck out of people, but I didn't know what that looked like or how to get there. Because of my love for God, at first I felt like I had to be involved heavily in the church, but I always said I didn't want to be stuck in a building every Wednesday and Sunday leading a small group. That wasn't the right thing for me because that's not where I connected the deepest with God. My church has always been found in sidewalk cracks and up in a big metal tube flying in the sky. The way I loved people best looked like people screaming at me about overhead bin space and Jesus teaching me about patience. It looked like me cleaning up waste from a man dying of cancer and holding a baby when a mother needed a break. It was all about me loving, never judging, and roaming full and free over every last corner of this earth. But during that conversation with my friend, I was reminded of that quote, and I realized what I had to do. I had to start with everything that was right in front of me.

At the time, my Instagram was growing, my deep desire for travel was growing, my love for capturing the beauty of my life was seeping out of my pictures, and I wanted others to feel it too. I realized I was actually turning into the person I wanted to be. I was becoming that brave, bold, beautiful wildflower of a lady. A travelin' lady. And I wanted to take all of my thoughts that wouldn't fit into an Instagram caption and place them somewhere others could access. Plus, I always loved taking pictures and had recently decided to start shooting film, so I thought, *Why don't I create a space to do that?*

I started a blog and named it *A Travelin' Lady*. It was born from a place of growing into the person I wanted to be and desperately looking for a way to lay out all of my passions, desires, favorite things, and love for others in one space. It is a project I am proud of, and it has kept growing with me.

When I first started my blog, it was simply that—a blog. I shared my favorite travels, skincare products, home renovations, and all of the fun stuff in between. I shared beautiful images from traveling, and heavy, vulnerable life moments as well. I never thought I would make money from it, but one day, it kind of just happened, and it was incredible. I started working with brands, companies, and even some tourism boards that sent me on really cool trips. All of this came from the simple desire to be light and Love to others and to share what made my life more hopeful and beautiful.

———————————

These days, my blog looks more like a showcase of all the beautiful moments in my life and from my travels. A virtual diary of sorts. I decided that since my greatest desire is to encourage and inspire others to get out there, what better way to do that than through travel guides? I collect all of my favorite spots, places to eat, places to stay, and sights to see, and create beautiful travel guides for others to use. One of the worst feelings is when you are getting ready to plan a trip and you are browsing Pinterest or Instagram, trying to find cool spots, then you find one but cannot find the name or location so you can go yourself. That has happened so many times to me, no matter how much detective work I do, and I wanted to help change that in a tiny way for others.

Sharing my images and travels is an incredible gift. It's a privilege to get thousands of likes and followers and have a blue check mark by my name. But what keeps me going, and my true purpose in all of this, is the chance to be Love to so many who need it deeply. My deepest desire is that people who come across my platform will have something spark inside of them. That they will get up from whatever they are stuck in and chase the beauty that is all around them. That they will know how much is out there for them. How much freedom is out there. How much healing is out there. How much kindness, beauty, grace, and love there is in the world.

When you first started this chapter and read the words "may your weeds be wildflowers," I bet it got you thinking. That little saying has stuck with me because I feel like a wildflower most days. I remember when I first started learning about myself and how I was designed, I felt like I had a lot of weeds that would never grow into something beautiful. As soon as I let go of trying to be like everyone else and started to walk my own path, they didn't feel like weeds; they felt like wildflowers. All the parts of me that made me, *me* were so beautiful. I listened to the deepest yearnings and desires in my heart and figured out how to make them a reality.

You can do what I did too. You can take all of your passions, desires, longings, and dreams and turn them into something for others. You can turn your weeds into beautiful wildflowers. What can you do today that will help you get there? Do you need to let go of a few things? Or maybe you need to get a few things to help you start. Whatever is on your heart that will help you share your light and love, you can do that. You can bring it up to the surface and make it real. If it's music, art, fashion, traveling, the outdoors, advocacy, cooking, anything that you are passionate about—it can be yours to give to others. It can be how you best connect with others and show them the goodness of Love. Figure out what keeps you up at night, and lean in to that. You were called to do so much with that beautiful life and passion of yours. I can't wait to see where it takes you.

i was sitting in row 9, seat F, wearing yoga pants and an old vintage T-shirt and rocking raccoon eyes from crying in the terminal bathroom. I could do things like that because I was young and going through a breakup and definitely didn't want to be on a flight to Portugal alone. Pushing yourself when your heart is bruised hurts.

I felt like too much of a mess to dig deep and go on some grand adventure. My joy felt stale; I felt stale. I felt like a failure because once again, I'd been dumped. I knew I needed to stop trying so hard to fix myself and to start accepting my flaws, finding my freedom in just that, but it was uncomfortable for me to push. But by getting on that flight, I was letting go of control.

That's what this trip was going to be for me. Getting out there on my own, on a solo trip to Europe, felt like getting as close to healing and Love as I possibly could. I walked into the trip not exactly sure why I was picking Portugal, but I knew it would open parts of my soul that needed to be cracked open. I knew I wouldn't be distracted. I knew I would be forced to spend precious time with myself and do some soul searching. I was scared but excited. I wasn't going into this trip just because my heart was bruised but because I knew I was made for more. I could see how parts of my soul had gotten tangled up in a mess of unhealthy relationships, craving love in an unhealthy way, and running away from my pain. It was time I stopped running or looking for distractions and started sitting with myself.

To this day, I still don't fully understand why I was absolutely petrified of traveling alone, but I was. Maybe I was afraid because I'd read scary news articles, heard horror stories from friends, or generally been told that it was a bad idea. Regardless, every chance I had to travel alone, I always backed out. Then one day I realized that solo travel was something I had to do. I was craving it. I needed it, even if it scared me deeply. Portugal is without a doubt my favorite place in the whole world. I picked Portugal as my first solo trip for that main reason. I had visited the year before with friends, so I was fairly familiar, and that made me a lot more comfortable.

You should know that the city of Lisbon is truly magical. There are countless winding, hilly, cobblestone roads with so many nooks and crannies to explore. The smell of pasta and seafood fills the air. There are street vendors selling sardines and Portugal's special pastry, *pastéis de nata*. In Portugal, the sun kisses your skin in a different kind of way, and the sky is the perfect shade of blue. You can go up a busy street and see mothers doing laundry and be enthralled by the plants hanging down from strangers' apartments. The tile art, called azulejo tiles, is out-of-this-world beautiful. Every building is filled with its own special tile. There's a special kind of magic in the air. You can just feel it.

I am a city girl at heart, don't get me wrong, but there is something healing about being near the sea for me. So during my trip, I decided to split my time between the cities of Lisbon and Faro, a beautiful beach town on the coast. I took a bus to Faro and checked into my room before I headed out to grab some food. That first night at dinner, I felt so alone. I ate my food with tears in my eyes. People eat alone all the time. Why was it so hard for me? Maybe I felt like it made me look out of place or like I didn't belong, and I never wanted to feel that way. Or maybe I loved being with other people so much that it reminded me of my singleness. Eventually I started to bring a notebook to journal and doodle in while I ate, and it made me feel a lot less alone.

I ended up making a few friends at the places I stayed. At night, everyone would come out to sit on the roof to talk. I made one friend named Julian, and our conversation stuck with me. Julian lived in Berlin, and we shared with each other why we both decided to go on our first solo travel trips. Turns out we both were running away from unhealthiness that had been going on in our worlds and were searching for something deeper, something more. A lot of our unhealthiness stemmed from relationships. It was nice being able to say "me too" with someone over and over again. Julian shared a lot with me, but the most memorable part of our short time together was him opening up about not being satisfied with where he was in his career. He shared a story about a billionaire in his neighborhood who had recently passed away. Julian said, "You know, when most wealthy people who pass away live empty lives and prioritize chasing money, they don't die wanting more money—they die wanting more time."

In that moment it dawned on me how much time we waste. We give so much time to unhealthiness and things that mean nothing to us. I don't want to leave this life begging for more time. Because the truth of the matter is, we have all the time in the world. Some might even say we have too much time.

At twenty-eight, I have as much time as I need. I think sometimes I just get in the pattern of wasting it. We stay stuck in the past and in the hurt and in the bitterness of what life offers us. We don't scoop up our freedom like we should. But we get to be in control. We get to pick the things we are living for and giving our hearts to every single day. Julian and I talked and shared more, but this conversation rattled me. I was wasting a lot of precious time on things that didn't matter. I needed to search deep and find the answers and find freedom. Hopefully Portugal would shine light on whatever that looked like.

As awkward as I felt most days because I kept overthinking being alone, I suddenly came to the realization that there was so much beauty around me I could focus on instead, and I wanted to dive into it, even if I took baby steps to get there. I found out there was a beach filled with one of my favorite things in this entire world: sea glass. I thought, *Instead of being sad that I have to walk down to the beach alone, what if I made it an adventure?* So that's just what I did. I spent my mornings waking up before the sun to walk down to the beach to collect sea glass and dance with the tide. It was magic dancing on the coast, finding handfuls of the most beautiful glass with the golden sun on my skin. Heading back into town, I would walk in the middle of the road and talk with God. Walking in the middle of the road is not the smartest idea, this I know, but when you are in a small European beach town, things like that don't really matter. Magic lives in doing things that don't fully make sense, and you do them because of it.

So as I was walking one morning, soaking up the immense beauty around me, I felt this heaviness weigh in, asking if I was living fully free. I was thrown off. Why would this matter? Why now? I was in the middle of a road in Portugal. Of course, I was living free. I thought I was, at least. Maybe it took something as simple as walking in the middle of the road in Portugal for me to realize that I was not giving my best, full self in other areas of life. I wanted badly to get out there and just walk without the brokenness or pain, but I realized that the pain and the brokenness are a beautiful part of my story. Maybe I wasn't meant to forgo the heaviness that has happened in my life but to carry it with me.

We are trained to feel ashamed of those things, aren't we? To hide our pain and brokenness unless it is appropriate to talk about them. Could you imagine a life where we showed up with the broken parts we would rather keep hidden and openly used them to grow forward? These simple words hit me in the middle of the road, and I still hold tight to them to this day: *I do not have to be fully fixed to live fully free.* That's what I came to Portugal to learn. I wasn't taking back a souvenir T-shirt or coffee mug; I was taking back one of the most freeing, beautiful life lessons. Traveling does that to you sometimes. It's a gift and a teacher—one I hope I never stop learning from.

The moments I had thought made me unqualified to live a life of full freedom didn't have the final say anymore. I could show up in my traveling, in my relationships, in my healing and find true freedom and joy. I didn't have to be this complete, put-together human. How many times have you thought that you couldn't do a certain thing because you weren't where you were supposed to be yet? Ask yourself if you really aren't ready or if it's just the insecurities of your hidden parts that are speaking louder than the truth. I'm not saying be irresponsible and do something you aren't ready for or push yourself to a spot you know you aren't supposed to be in. What I'm saying is, quiet down that voice that speaks from your broken parts and choose a life of freedom and courage even when you don't feel like it. You do not have to be put together to experience joy. You do not have to be fully fixed from all your brokenness in order to live fully free.

———

Before my trip, I had been wrapped up in so many things. I let my anxiety and depression dictate my every move. My joy couldn't exist because I let my circumstances take control of my reality. I couldn't break free; I didn't have the courage to. Maybe it was okay to feel heavy, but I didn't have to sit in that heaviness. I could get back up and chase down the freedom I so heavily wished for.

If I wouldn't have stepped out and gone to Portugal, I wouldn't have learned such important things that have shaped me so deeply. If I had turned around in the airport and listened to the broken parts of me like I so desperately wanted to when I was sobbing in that terminal bathroom, I would have missed out on my solo trip where God showed up in the most simple, profound ways.

Despite the doubts I had in myself and my growth, my fears of being truly honest with myself, the heartache I carried from my breakup, and the awkwardness that I experienced during my week of traveling in Portugal alone, I got much more out of it than I could have ever hoped for. It shaped me as a person, and it set new ground in my steps moving forward. I got to look my fears straight in the eye and ask what they really were and how I could replace them. And all this forward momentum started by my showing up.

You can do that too; you can show up for yourself. You can look at yourself honestly—as scary as that might be—and dig deep down into the parts of you that scare you. The parts you would rather hide away high up on the shelf. The broken parts that make you run away from light, joy, and freedom. You can start there and call them out. It doesn't have to be an intense thing. You can pull them out, show them to God with palms up, and say, "Can you take this for me? Can we get through this together?" And you don't have to be alone in Portugal to do this. You can be in your car, on your bed, at work, or wherever you feel like your journey needs to start.

This is what I will say on traveling alone: do it. Do it now, do it next week, do it next year, and do it until you are eighty. No matter who is in your world or if you are in love or lonely or sad or happy or mad, go pack up your bags and get out there. Book a flight to wherever the light can get in and stir up things in your soul. Go scared, and go find out how to be brave. Don't do it for Instagram photos or for a cool blog post. Don't do it to run away either—do it to find out more about yourself. Don't worry about your hair or your smelly armpits. Get lost. Feel uncomfortable in your first couple of days alone. But keep your chin up and realize that the trip is more than a lonely meal or a lonely trip; it's tasting freedom in such a real way.

When you want to get to know someone, you spend time investing in them. It should be a rule for your own soul too. When you travel alone, you will learn more about yourself and your capabilities than you think is possible. I promise you. Go. Don't look back. Fighting for yourself when you really don't want to is a scary thing, but goodness, it is always worth it. When we listen to the truth instead of fear, we grow. So, can I tell you the truth one more time? You do not have to be fully fixed to live fully free. Hold that close as you leave these pages. Write it on your mirror or put it on your phone background. Can you do that for me? There is so much goodness and beauty waiting for you out there. You still have time to become, and you don't have to waste another second of your life waiting to feel that freedom. Go out and find it. It's all around you.

d id you know that I cannot recall one single time I have been afraid to be on an airplane? Even through the worst turbulence and flying often as an unaccompanied minor, I was never scared. Fun fact, by the way: I live for turbulence! Most people call me crazy when I tell them that, but I love flying and everything that comes along with aviation. It's one of the greatest joys of my life. My stepmom, Amy, on the other hand, can be a nervous flyer. So to this day, the one and only person besides me who has done a "words from the window seat" that I have shared is my stepmom. She got creative with her note, too, putting mine to shame. Her note read, "Take a smile," with tiny pull-off strips of smiles like those tear-off flyers you see at coffee shops. When I was growing up, my stepmom always told us to love everyone and be kind always, so I thought it was beautiful that she would share a note despite being uncomfortable. I knew how much peace it brought her up in the air to leave a note for a stranger. To practice that kindness she always taught us about, even when she was not in the most comfortable spot.

———

Do you know what has really scared me, though? Working on my relationship with my dad and stepmom. I know that sounds weird and selfish, but it is hard for anyone to look at the people who have brought them pain and say, "Hey, let's fix this together." We are beautiful, complex, and complicated human beings. All messy, all with scars, and all with stories to tell. For a long time now, my dad and biological mom have been the cause of much heaviness in my becoming. From divorcing when I was too young to understand, to getting remarried before I was ready, to unhealthy relationships that I witnessed, and my biological mother not being in my life, a lot happened to me that has dramatically shaped and changed who I am as a person. Most of the qualities I walked away with from childhood are ones I wish hadn't stuck around.

Now, as a twenty-eight-year-old, I'm figuring out a lot of important life lessons. Like the fact that even though I may not have had a say when I was six years old, I can sit down with myself today and say, "Okay, Tay, what qualities do we have here that need to go?" Once I name the unhealthy qualities out loud, they begin to lose their power. I can prioritize doing the work. Therapy has been my guardian angel. So much inner work has happened because of continually going to therapy. I've spent a lot of time recalling my childhood and rewriting the story and the trauma for myself. Instead of seeing how my parents' divorce made me feel unloved and unwanted, I get to say that it's made me softer and more in tune with others' pain. Instead of feeling the hurt and rejection of not having a relationship with my biological mom, I get to say that I am going to work extra hard at having a healthy relationship with my future children. One of the most beautiful things Jesus gives us with redemption is the ability to rewrite.

The more work I put into healing from my childhood, the more clarity I get on this life I have been given. The weight of being scared to work on my relationship with my parents becomes lighter. I start to see them as human beings carrying their own scars and joys instead of super-heroes or villains. The older I get, the more grace and love I have for them; the more I want to reach out and hug them with all I've got.

I blamed my stepmom for a long time because she was an easy target. She was the one who stepped up to take care of us and who was mostly around when my dad worked long hours to provide for us. Blaming her felt easier than dealing with all the built-up pain. But I have had this beautiful realization over the last few years that she did the best she could with what she had. She loved us and raised us despite everything. I wouldn't be where I am today without her. I made the choice to put my pain aside one day and invite her in. And what better way to do that than to spend four days driving in a U-Haul? We were going to go on an epic, cross-country road trip and, hopefully, grow our relationship.

———————

I had always dreamed of living in California; I just never thought it would be possible for me as a flight attendant. The main airport in Los Angeles, LAX, is one of the hardest bases to transfer into because a lot of flight attendants never leave the base. I didn't know exactly where I wanted to live in California, but I knew that Los Angeles was a huge airport that I was very interested in flying out of. They have flights to Sydney, all of Hawaii, Asia, and a lot of other incredible places I'd always dreamed of visiting.

One day, sitting in my Chicago apartment, I got the news that LAX was taking one hundred and fifty flight attendants, and I immediately put my name on the transfer list. I found out a few weeks later that my transfer was granted—I would be flying out of LAX in just a few short months. I was over the moon excited! I had been living in Chicago for almost four years and was ready to be outside rock climbing and camping; I was ready for a change. Over the next few months, I said my goodbyes and decided to ask my stepmom if she wanted to fly in and do the move with me. I knew it would be good for her and for our relationship, and I couldn't think of anyone better to have by my side. The day before the big drive, I had my apartment all packed up in a moving van and was ready to hit the open road.

I will never forget picking Amy up in that huge U-Haul at Chicago O'Hare International Airport. I pulled up to Terminal 3, hopped out of the big rig, and unlocked the back to slide up the door to store her luggage. We were laughing and smiling from the first moment our adventure started. I probably looked so tiny driving the U-Haul, but it was my dream come true.

We set off toward the interstate to get us to St. Louis and then to Oklahoma where we would spend the night. Within the first few hours, we decided to name our moving van Bertha because it just felt right. Over the next few days, we listened to a lot of country music and enjoyed miles and miles of wide-open spaces. We stopped in Albuquerque, New Mexico, to see all the scenes from Amy's favorite TV show, *Breaking Bad*. We stopped in Holbrook, Arizona, to see these incredible hotel rooms shaped like tepees. We drove a few hours out of the way to see the Grand Canyon. We even got stopped and searched at a California border protection station because of all the plants I had brought with me from Chicago.

Every time Bertha made a horribly frightening noise, we just looked at each other and laughed. I don't know what it was about the trip, but everything was beautiful, funny, and full of so much joy. We couldn't stop smiling. Maybe it was because we were rewriting. Maybe it was the fumes from Bertha, I really don't know. What I do know is that I will always hold this adventure with my stepmom close. It was such a special trip because this was the start to healing our relationship. This was the first time in my life that I saw my stepmom as a human being who just needed love like the rest of us and not as someone who should be a perfect parent. Even though we didn't have a relationship-altering conversation on the road trip, it was a start for both of us. It brought us together, and that was something. We just needed that first step, and it was a beautiful one.

———————

I am so proud of the woman Amy has helped me become. I wouldn't be where I am today without her. Our relationship is still a work in progress, just like all relationships. I felt it important to share about my relationships with my parents because I think those relationships are some of the biggest sources of hurt and joy in most of our lives. For me, these relationships have taken work and understanding—a lot of grace and a whole lot of love.

Have you ever taken the time to sit back and realize the pain that your upbringing may have caused you? I'm not talking about playing the victim but about realizing that things may have happened to you as a child that you didn't have a say in then but have a say in now. Have you had that realization yet that your parents aren't superheroes? They are human beings who need love and grace just as much as you do. I'm not sure where you come from or what your parent or family dynamic looks like, but if that relationship is heavy for you, I am deeply sorry. And I get it in some ways, I truly do. But can I say this? Maybe you are who you are because of who they weren't. Maybe one day you are going to be the best mother or father due to a lack or absence of one in your life. Maybe you are going to be gentle and soft because your father was hard and stern. Or maybe you will be the best communicator because you didn't have that from your parents. I know it's hard to see, but it's there waiting for you. Pinkie promise. Until then, continue to throw love and grace around, as hard as it may be. Relationships are so much lighter that way.

I think back to the note my stepmom left while being a nervous, anxious flyer, and it makes sense even in regard to our relationship and to the bigger picture. She was doing the best she could with what she had right in that very moment on the airplane, probably like she did when I was growing up. Flawed, nervous, and just doing the best she could every day. That right there is a reason to take a smile.

O ne time I flew four thousand miles overseas to stay with complete strangers. Okay, maybe I shouldn't say *complete* strangers. We had one mutual friend who I knew from the internet, but they were pretty much strangers to me. A few months prior to my trip, we had started following each other on Instagram. Jess sent me the kindest message explaining she'd had a vivid dream about me and insisted that I come to visit her and her family in Barcelona. I always tell people to be careful about inviting me to their home for an adventure because I will always show up. So, that's exactly what I did. Shortly after she sent an invite, I was ringing her doorbell in Spain.

From the minute I landed in Barcelona and started roaming around, I was in love. The first thing I did after meeting everyone in person and setting my stuff down was grab a skateboard and head out the door. (Oh yeah, this trip to Barcelona was going to be spent with a bunch of skateboarders.) Talk about a dream come true. I have been skating for years. (Mostly cruising, don't get too excited.)

Within the first couple of hours of arriving, I had already made five new friends. I spent my next days skateboarding, exploring all the different parts that Barcelona had to offer, eating all I could manage, over-caffeinating, and having a lot of deep talks with Jess. I quickly realized that my new friend was a lot like me. She had fought beautifully and bravely with mental health, and she and her husband, Shaun, are incredible. They love Jesus in such a raw, real way.

Sitting with her one morning, sharing about my faith, anxiety, depression, and so many other things that usually feel awkward to share, really made it click that I was finally doing okay. I had finally gotten to a healthy, good place. We grow and share where we feel safe, don't we? When I first started writing this book, I didn't know how I was going to write a chapter about my mental health. It's the hardest struggle for me to put into words for many reasons. This trip was special because opening up and talking with someone who has fought so similarly to me made it easier for the words to come out. As I sat there and wrote from a Barcelona café covered in plants, with the sun hugging me, I felt courageous enough to get these words out. I felt strong enough and far enough along in my healing and understanding to speak up. Being in Barcelona was my way of letting my heart air out. It felt so good.

———————

As I've shared before, I started struggling with anxiety and depression when I was six years old. I never felt safe enough, or understood enough, to tell anyone about it. I just suppressed my feelings and didn't understand that they had a name until I was in my twenties. I'd carried depression and anxiety around like bricks in a backpack my whole life. They were always with me, always speaking for me, always stealing, always controlling so much of who I was.

I could share a million specific stories of what anxiety and depression have looked like for me, but it's so hard to put into words. I can simply tell you that panic attacks feel like having your breath stolen from you and dry heaving. Your whole body tingles, aches, and burns. Anxiety feels like the worst-case scenario is happening in your life, whether is a reality or not. You have to fight and hold on for dear life to save yourself. More times than not, the things I was anxious about, ended up being things that worked out fine in the end. That still doesn't stop the anxiety from coming. It's a coping mechanism in a way. But depression is sneaky. Depression is as sly as a fox and as smooth as a snake. It is such a tenacious beast that loves to act as a friend. Depression finds your sore spots and runs wild with them. Depression is so good at lying and twisting your reality into something that it's not. I can still taste the metallic on my tongue when I think about depression.

After getting out of my first unhealthy relationship, I fell hard. I struggled with heightened anxiety, depression, self-harm, and suicide. Writing that down on paper makes me sad for the girl I used to be. I just had no idea how much better it could get. For so long, this was the weight I carried. Though I carried it well, I was always the burdened girl. By God's grace, I met Jesus when I needed hope, help, and healing the most. I started my work healing and understanding, but it did not happen overnight. If you are struggling with any of these things, please reach out and get help. There are resources in the back of this book for you to use. There are doctors, therapists, medicines, and workouts that can help too.

For a very, very long time, I felt guilty about loving God while also struggling with deep mental health issues. Since meeting Jesus, I have been taught that I am not to worry, have anxiety, or stress about the things I cannot control. While all of this is true and important, where does that leave me—the girl with years of suppressed depression, anxiety, and stress? These things are embedded into my bones. I've gone up for healing prayers. I've gotten on my hands and knees and begged to be "normal." I've tried so many times to do the best I can to handle and trust when life is happening. It is a hard, teeth-gritting kind of work.

I'm not fully there yet. I still wake up and have issues that are going to take time to figure out and heal from. There was a time I decided to get on medication to try and help. After a few different trial-and-error runs with finding the right medication, I finally found the right one. Let me tell you here first if you haven't heard it before: *that is okay*. I didn't know what was the right way to go about things or how I was supposed to get better without feeling guilty all of the time. I want you to know that there is no reason to feel guilty. No matter what the world tells you, or what the church tells you, or what your family tells you, it is your journey and yours alone.

One of the most important things I have learned throughout my journey is that vulnerability and healing go hand in hand with my mental health fight. Vulnerability is so important. As much as I have wanted to stay hidden and not burden people with my pain, it is one of the most important aspects of healing. Asking for help at the beginning felt like having to do karaoke; not only am I absolutely horrible at it, but it's also my deepest fear. I started letting others in by sharing snippets of my fight on the internet and making new friends whom I trusted to help me carry my pain. I used to be so bad about that, but I learned people make the healing more beautiful and less terrifying when we let them into our pain.

In the midst of my most broken and darkest nights, I started reaching out. I might have been quiet as a mouse, but I reached, and people kept showing up for me. They said I was loved, worthy, and beautiful, and I believed them. No matter what my depression was telling me or what lies were being fed to me, I chose to believe the people speaking into my pain. I had friends who would come sit in my bed and hold me when I cried. I had friends who would sit on my front stoop and not leave until I opened the door. Things got lighter and started to shift because I fought for them. I fought as hard as I could alongside these friends. I also stopped feeling guilty and sad for myself all of the time, and I started diving in deep and hard on what was true in my life. Now vulnerability feels like courage. Vulnerability feels like putting on my superhero cape and fighting for the things that truly matter.

I started learning what Jesus said about me. He said that I am beautiful and wonderful. Fearfully made. He knew what he was doing when he made *me*. I can run to him, and I can trust him. So you know what? I started to do just that. And layers started to peel back. I stopped feeling guilty for showing up messy and started to celebrate simply showing up and putting in the work. It stopped feeling impossible to heal and felt easier to trust and grow. I signed up for therapy regularly. I read books that challenged my healing. I worked. I fought. I cried. I took four steps forward and three steps back. Over and over again. You know what? After years of doing this and understanding myself more, the pain got lighter. My mental health is my friend, not my own worst enemy. We are working together with a lot of love and grace to figure this thing out. There is no shame or guilt or fear. There is just honesty and a better understanding of something I didn't take the time to understand.

I trained my mind for so long to always be ready to carry the heaviest load. For the longest time, I was waiting for things to shift. For me to finally feel healthier. For the load to get lighter in my life because, goodness, it was a nightmare most days. I realized I was putting pressure on myself to be somewhere that took time and steps to reach. So I stopped putting pressure on myself to be healthier and better and started doing the work of self-care. It took a lot of consistency. It takes believing that there are *truly* brighter days ahead—even in the midst of heaviness and on days where you can't pull yourself out of bed. In a conversation about mental health where I was talking as fast as the Road Runner, a friend nudged me and said these words, "Hold it lightly, love; one day at a time." Those words have proven to be powerful for me.

———

The weight of struggling with mental health issues is real. It is hard not to shut down and beat myself up for failing daily. As I have learned to hold it lightly and truly put that into practice, the crazy thing is, it does feel lighter. I think it's important to be honest with my mental health battle. Do I hold it lightly every single time I have a feeling of anxiety, stress, or depression? Absolutely not. Is it the hardest, most challenging part about being a human and choosing healthiness? You bet. It's hard to tell someone how they are supposed to feel and what they should do when it comes to mental health. This chapter is mostly here so that you might not feel so alone in your fight. There are many incredible resources out there to help you on your journey. My journey has looked like having a strong support system, attending therapy, finding the right medications, understanding my relationship with God deeper, and doing a whole lot of inner work; as many times as it takes.

I want you to know that I genuinely love you. The world needs your story and for you to fight. Once you get through what feels like your world shattering, you are going to come out so much stronger and more beautiful. People need to hear that story. If you are heavy and need someone who will listen and can help you carry your pain, reach out to someone. Dig down deep and fight. Remember to hold it lightly, love. One day at a time.

a s I was standing in the middle of the airplane aisle, waiting for the next cue in the safety demonstration, I saw a tiny little hand shoot up in the air. I could tell from far away that he was holding on to some sort of treasure. *Did he find something on the floor or was he just being a normal, playful kid?* I had to find out. I inched closer, peeked over the seat, and realized he was holding something small between his two little fingers. This precious little boy was actually holding a tooth he'd just lost. This was a first. I had never seen anyone in my seven years of being a flight attendant light up like that, let alone lose a tooth. The mom looked at me giggling and said, "I'm going to label this one 'airplane tooth.'"

These are the moments I hold close. I still believe deeply in the beauty and magic of life. In these little moments that happen when we slow down to see them. When we believe in them and count the little things just as important as the others. Maybe it wasn't a big deal that someone lost their tooth that day on the runway, but to me it was. Things can be all the more special when we have the wonder in our hearts to let them. This moment reminds me of another beautiful moment, one I had while I was in the bed of a pickup truck in a herd of wild buffalo. Let me explain.

When I'm not flying in the friendly skies, I sometimes get freelance work from my Instagram or blog. A lot of the freelance jobs involve using my love for words, photography, and traveling. Even though I don't get jobs often, it's a lot of fun and another way I get to express myself. There was an email sitting in my inbox one morning about a new potential freelance job. One that involved traveling, national parks, and a big adventure. I barely read through the whole email before I sent my "count me in" response back. I realized as I read more that the project was in South Dakota. It's a state I don't hear of or think about often, and I immediately started to google images and things to do there. There wasn't much popping up besides big tourist spots, but that was okay. I decided I was going to go for it anyway. I can never turn down an adventure.

I touched down in one of those teeny tiny planes at the Rapid City Regional Airport on an extremely rainy South Dakota day. I headed off to grab my rental car and immediately started my adventure. The people who'd hired me had given me a list of all the spots around town, so I felt like I had a cheat sheet to the magic.

I started off my first day visiting a horse sanctuary. I am a huge animal lover, and any place that protects animals is dear to my heart. The sweetest cowboy drove us all over the hills, teaching us about the horses, the protected land, and Indigenous culture. The horses were beautiful and roamed free, and that kind of beauty does something to you. I said a lot of thank-yous to those at the horse sanctuary and to the earth beneath my feet. I had a feeling that South Dakota was already starting to teach me an important life lesson.

When I woke up the next day, I saw white out of my window. I realized I was seeing South Dakota's first snow of the season, which I was over the moon about but also had not prepared for. Today was the big day! It was the buffalo roundup. I know the term *buffalo roundup* sounds strange, but that's exactly what it is: a roundup of buffalo. It's part of the state park's plan to maintain a healthy balance between the number of buffalo and the land that is available for them. They use a group of twenty cowboys—picked from a lottery—to actually handle the buffalo and herd them. These cowboys also check the health of the herd, making sure they have the proper vaccinations and that the pregnant ladies are doing fine.

Before the roundup started, I had the pleasure of meeting Bob, the oldest and longest-riding cowboy in the roundup. Bob was eighty-five years old and told me that he had been riding in the roundup for forty-three years and was proud to be there another year. I was absolutely starstruck and asked him if he wanted to be my boyfriend. He was covered in cowboy gear and smelled like leather. I spent quite a few moments with him listening to his story and feeling so at home. I was covered in mud, freezing cold, and my phone was tucked away, but I was there living.

After talking with Bob, the group I was with loaded up in truck beds. The roundup was held at Custer State Park, where over twenty thousand people came to watch from the sidelines. There are only about ten trucks allowed in the actual roundup area following the herd, and the other thousands of spectators watch from the top of the hills. I felt so lucky. As I was holding on in the back of the truck looking up at the thousands of people watching from the sidelines, I realized this was a once-in-a-lifetime experience. I couldn't believe that I got to be a part of it.

We set off with the cowboys, who rode on horseback, to try to find the buffalo grazing in the park. The buffalo were being stubborn at first, and the cowboys had a hard time getting them to the proper area to start the roundup. Then the cowboys sped off, and we knew it was showtime. I honestly had no idea what to expect, I just knew I was in the back of a pickup truck making friends and about to see some buffalo. Once we turned the corner and the mountain that had been blocking the view of the buffalo faded, I instantly started crying. I had never experienced anything like what I was seeing in my life. The mountains were far off, acting as the backdrop all around me, and the rolling hills were sprinkled with light snow from the night before. We were far away from the main area, so there were no spectators around, which made the moment even more special and quiet. It was just a few trucks, cowboys on horses, and thousands—I mean thousands—of wild buffalo right in front of me. The first words out of my mouth were "I am going to tell my children about this one day!" I was so excited. We followed the buffalo as I held on for dear life in the back of the truck. I took some pictures, but for the most part, I put my phone and camera down. I had to soak it all in. I could not believe the beauty that was in front of me. I will cherish that day and that moment of being so immersed in wild, pure beauty for a long time to come.

I'm a cowgirl at heart, no doubt about it. I love being outside, getting dirty, camping, you name it. Maybe as I was telling you this buffalo story, you were thinking, *This one is not for me.* For a second, imagine the most beautiful moment in your life that you can think of. Do you remember being on your phone or the outfit you wore to get you likes during this moment? Or do you remember how the beauty made you feel? Do you remember how your breathing felt different and you felt lighter? Being in the back of that truck in the middle of South Dakota was that moment for me. Holding on for dear life, I realized that I don't need more things—I just need more beauty.

Are you attached to your phone most days? Or obsessed with how many likes your selfie gets? How many times do you redo your talking Instagram stories to make sure they're just right or that your bad side isn't showing? How many things have you bought without thinking it through because one of your favorite people on the internet advertised it? Our generation is wrapped up in junk we don't need. Stuff that won't even matter someday. Isn't that crazy? We spend so much time trying to impress others when there are many other more important things to put ourselves into. I share a lot of beautiful things on the internet, but my biggest hope is not to impress the socks off of anyone but to inspire and ignite something deep inside someone else. I feel called to share this beautiful life I get to live and all the beautiful places I get to experience.

Traveling is one of the most freeing and important things you can do for yourself. It really, truly is. And if you walk away from this book knowing that, I've done my job. The most beautiful, encouraging thing is that travel doesn't have to always be across the sea or cost thousands of dollars. You can have an adventure in your own backyard or the state next door. This idea that I don't need more things, just more beauty, has dug deep into my being. My closet looks different now. My bank account is breathing a lot freer. This huge weight of trying to impress people has shifted to only wanting to love them. It's more than just my closet or bank account, though. I've found my freedom too.

—————

As the truck pulled back up to end the roundup, I got out and headed straight toward my car to find a dirt road. I took it all the way to Badlands National Park where the smell of wild sage filled the air. I found a place to pull over to dance with the wind during golden hour—just me and my freedom. We looked beautiful together. God was there, too, because I could see him in all the beauty that surrounded me. I took a deep breath in and a deep breath out. This was the beauty I needed.

I hope so far that you've laughed, maybe cried a little, felt more understood, and learned a thing or two through all my notes and stories. This specific chapter, though, is really important. I have a lot of things to say about love and relationships, sadly, because I've had a lot of bad ones. I mean a lot. It took me a really long time to love healthily and to find the kind of love I needed. I convinced myself that I would never find it either. Not someone like me.

I remember my first love like it was yesterday. He was the quarterback of a high school football team, an all-around jock who drove a big blue pickup truck. Just to clarify, I was not *that* girl in high school. You know, the popular cheerleader who ends up with the quarterback. I was a track and distance runner who worked at an ice cream shop and babysat all the neighborhood kids on the weekends. I was the girl in high school who tried to be friends with everyone. I still don't know how I ended up with Mr. Popular, but I guess he saw something in my quirks.

Our song was some corny Taylor Swift ballad, and even though I thought ours was a picture-perfect love, I knew deep down it wasn't. Looking back now, ten years older and wiser, I can call out that I was searching to be loved unconditionally, understood, and safe with someone. It's all I ever wanted. Yes, this is a basic need for most humans searching for love, but for me, it was much more. Being loved was how I thought I would be healed. It was how I tried to patch up old wounds that never got the chance to heal properly. It was like medicine in the wound left by my absent mother. It was the thread I used to stitch up the scar my father left by always being at work and never taking the time to get to know me. As a seventeen-year-old developing girl, I thought I had finally perfected the art of healing. I was going to use love and relationships to mend and become. To love is to heal, isn't it? Oh, how wrong and unhealthy I was.

My first love ended quickly and abruptly, as love often does when one or both humans aren't healthy or ready for love. Let me tell you, being dumped absolutely crushed me. It was so much deeper than a breakup. The walls that had been concealing and holding up years of pain came crashing down. I was not mentally ready for the blow. I spent many weeks depressed, struggling with self-harm, and fighting suicidal thoughts. And you know what? Not one person knew. Not my parents or my friends. No one. I carried the load quietly and desperately.

One day I finally caved and talked to a friend, Meredith. I didn't give her all the details, but I told her just enough. She invited me to church, and for whatever reason, I went. It was unlike any church I had ever been to, even though I could count the number of times I had been to church on one hand. A few weeks later, I met Jesus. I dove headfirst into all of the beautiful things that come with knowing Jesus, but only for a little while. Before I knew it, there was another boy sweeping me off my feet.

I had years, and I mean *years*, of ignored pain and trauma. It was shoved down deep. That kind of pain and trauma takes time to work through. The process takes therapy and sometimes medication. It involves a lot of grace and a lot of space. I had my faith, of course, and that came with a lot of clarity, joy, and closer steps to becoming the person I wanted to be. But I sadly still thought it was okay to keep throwing myself into relationships, and I did that as many times as I could. All I wanted was to love and be loved so desperately, so badly, that it didn't matter what I needed to heal from. To love was to heal. So I thought.

———

I ran around the love mountain over and over and over again in my teens and early twenties. I went from one unhealthy relationship to another. All the while, I was still the same unhealthy Taylor. I would do a few counseling sessions when things got bad, and then I would never go back. Depression and anxiety were always there, but I called them "not enough sleep" or "stressed from work." I never let any friends get close enough to help me or even get to know the real me. All I wanted or could see was love. It was my addiction of choice. Getting married. Finally being enough for someone who would stick around to love me unconditionally. I loved wrong for a very long time.

Eventually I found someone who was just as unhealthy as I was, and he stuck around—for what reason, I'm still unsure. That relationship was filled with sadness and brokenness; even writing it now, I have to forgive myself over and over again. Even though I walked into the relationship unhealthy and with such a wrong perception of what love looked like, I stayed and became an even uglier version of myself. I was so broken that I thought marriage would make all my pain go away. He proposed in the most magical way, and I said yes.

We set a date, planned the wedding out perfectly, and I bought my dream dress. Not one person knew how heavy things were when it was just us and social media wasn't watching. One day the facade finally came crashing down. I found myself sitting on top of a dryer doing laundry in my apartment's shared laundry room. My fiancé and I were miles apart, talking on the phone casually, when all of a sudden we got into a major argument, which really caught me off guard. There was talk of taking a week to think about how to move forward and figure out what we wanted or if getting married was truly the right thing. I couldn't breathe. If I was not going to be married and be loved forever, what was I going to be?

I freaked out. I said and thought the most bizarre, unstable things. I couldn't be alone or sit still for a whole week while I waited to see what was going to happen. I called our friends who lived a few hours away who knew us both and decided to spend some time at their house processing. I wasn't planning on telling them the whole truth, though, because once the words left my mouth about what was going on in our relationship, I could never get them back. They spent a few days listening and telling me it was probably just cold feet, everything would be okay. I nodded my head and reassured myself that this argument would pass; everything would be fine after we talked when the week was up.

Then one night it was just the girls, and we were having our normal conversation where I worked through all of my thoughts and fears. There was a pause, and this feeling came over me. To this day, I have still never felt anything like it. I think it was God, to be fully honest with you. I felt him say, *Taylor, this is not it.* It took one second for all of the feelings and truths I was hiding away to be released. I knew our relationship wasn't right. I knew it was terribly wrong to lie and settle for something so broken, and I knew I couldn't get married with such unhealthy tendencies. I immediately told my friend the whole truth about our relationship and felt so much peace. The days after that were a blur. I went back home with a firm decision to say no to a wedding and to an unhealthy relationship, no matter what kind of conversations I had moving forward. And I did just that.

Even after going through all of that, I still tried to continue the cycle of unhealthy relationships in my life. I still made really bad decisions and was not the person I wanted to be. I got to a healthy place eventually—it just took me a long time to get to a place where I genuinely said no to using relationships as Band-Aids for my wounds.

A lot of that growth came with time and making better decisions for myself. It came from surrounding myself with beautiful, healthy people and relationships that allowed me to open up and be honest. The more I shared with people about wrong stuff going on in relationships, the more they taught me what good, healthy love should look like. It wasn't just me making decisions with my emotions and heart anymore like I used to when I held all my relational pain inside. I had people to honestly tell me, "Hey I don't think this is okay or what should be happening in a healthy relationship."

I also started working on myself, and I figured out what made me, me without someone else by my side. I pushed hard into healing, traveling, therapy, figuring out my mental health, and being honest deep down. It was work. It took a lot of lonely days and tears. It took a lot of digging deep and realizing how unhealthy I had been for years. I stopped playing the victim, and I started doing the work to heal.

I share these past relationship experiences not because I am a sad girl who needs to get revenge or because I am still holding on to pain or unforgiveness. In fact, I've been extremely hesitant to even share this part of my life because I truly don't want to hurt anyone's character or cause pain in others' lives. Even though I suffered as a result of others' unhealthy habits and brokenness, I was just as broken, unhealthy, and manipulative as they were. I had such little respect for myself and for my future that I would do whatever it took to make unhealthy love work. I was absolutely desperate. I ate, slept, inhaled, and craved love. I spent so much time during the most important years of my growing life on dysfunctional relationships.

That's why I feel it's important now for me to speak back on them. To speak for my past self; she was never strong enough or healthy enough to say these things. I share these extremely vulnerable moments in hopes that you will hear me, learn from my mistakes, look deep inside yourself, and ask, *What's motivating my need for love?* What is it? Ask yourself, then look at the current or past relationships in your life. What do they look like?

What do they bring you? What do you bring to them? Are you *finding* healthy love or *manipulating* love to fill you up in some unhealthy way?

If I can help one human reading this not settle or get out of an unhealthy relationship or pause on entering a relationship due to your own unhealthiness, then it will all have been worth it. If any part of you aches or relates while reading my experiences with love, this is for you. If you feel like you are substituting relationships for healing, let's be honest with ourselves now. I promise you, from experience, substitution will only end in pain. You will never be fulfilled. You will never feel good enough, and you will most likely run around the mountain surrounded by love, over and over again, until you learn. Let's take a deep breath together. I'm proud of you for making it this far. I'm so proud.

Maybe you are someone who can't currently relate. Maybe you've found a healthy kind of love. Maybe you've walked through this already and taken that beautiful time to heal. I am so proud of you. Truly. How brave you must be. It's so important, though, that we have this moment together because there are so many who still need to create a plan or open up to a loved one for the first time about getting help or getting out of a relationship. Or maybe we all just need to celebrate our past selves. They have taught us so much, haven't they? Let's sit in that for a minute. Take a deep breath. We will be okay.

———————

I've come a long way since my early twenties when I needed love to breathe. I've taken the time to heal. I go to therapy regularly so that I can better understand trauma and how it affects my life. I understand my mental health and myself more than I ever have. I've forgiven myself and others as many times as it takes. I also don't play the victim, and I take responsibility for my unhealthiness too. I know Jesus deeply, and I know his love and goodness to be oh so true. I see it every day. In the wildflowers and in the sidewalk cracks.

I've even met the sweetest of loves. His name is Joseph. He gave me a shiny diamond ring on my left finger. I am loved deeper than I knew possible. I am understood more than I have ever been in my whole life. I am better because of Joseph, every single day. I am finally experiencing the healthy, stable kind of love. This is what I am learning about the healthy kind of love: it's the best kind of growing pain I have yet known. When we have arguments, I'm not threatened or disrespected. I'm loved unconditionally. I'm understood immensely. He reads articles about anxiety and how to love your loved ones who struggle. He holds my hand when I cry and cries with me too. He writes songs about me and our love.

He's all I could have ever wanted or dreamed of, but if I'm being honest, I never thought guys like him really existed. I thought they were all taken or married already. I still can't believe I found him. I can't believe I get to love someone like Joseph and be loved in return. We are learning a lot about love together.

But as beautiful as my love is with Joseph, I continue to grow from a place of unlearning. It's really, really hard work that I wish I would have saved myself from. I get down on myself so much and wish I would have said no, waited until I was healthy enough, and walked away from past relationships. I find myself feeling like I wasted so much time with people who should have never gotten to have those years and moments. I am retraining my brain to speak goodness over myself even though I have failed before. I can be my own worst enemy sometimes. But this all is a part of my story. It's a story that led me to Joseph, and together, I know we can change the world. We can help a lot of beautiful people and their beautiful relationships.

I look back sometimes and can't believe I'm the me I am now because I sure as heck am nowhere near the broken girl I used to be. I made so many different versions of myself for so long to fit someone else's need for me to be a certain way. I never thought I'd get here. I never thought someone would stay. I really thought another human being sticking with me was rocket science. Please know love is out there for you. I'm not sure how many times you've told yourself you are going to end up alone, but I promise with my whole heart that it's not true. No matter how far off and unreal it may seem, you have to keep walking away from the love that is stale toward the love that is true. You can't settle. You have to keep growing into the best version of yourself on your own. Keep coming home to yourself, and I promise you, love will show up. You were made to love and be loved.

———

As I wrap up this chapter, I'm sitting on an early morning flight, where all of my creative magic happens, and I see a barf bag peeking out of the seat-back pocket in front of me. (I know; I am a fancy published author, and I called it a barf bag. But that's just what I call it, okay?) Big, bold letters that say WASTE are staring at me. And I'm thinking, *Well, that's rude. Waste* is such a forward word, yet how often do I use that word toward myself? How many times have I spoken over myself that I wasted so much time getting into unhealthy messes? Better yet, how many men have told me that they wasted time on me?

Waste. The word rings loud, and it's up to me to quiet it down. I'm realizing in this beautiful moment that I have not wasted my love. Ever. Did you hear that? Let me tell you again. You did not waste your love. Ever. A poet I love, Amy Turn Sharp, wrote those words. And yes, they were meant for you too.

I've been wounded deeply from relationships. Deep-freaking-ly. I know I have wounded others as well. The pain from heartbreak has been the hardest thing I've walked through in this life, but it's also been the most beautiful. My goodness, has it been beautiful. It's shaped me into who I am and how I love. It's made the pockets of my heart so much deeper and more open. I know how hard it is to look at past love and think it wasn't a waste, but I promise you one day everything will make sense. Learn from the broken. Let the pain push you forward. Let it crack open the deepest parts of your soul for love to get in. The good kind of love.

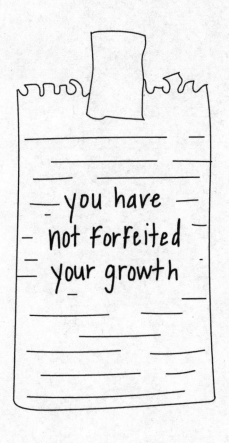

d id you know that I have been working on this book for over four years now? I've had two different agents, two different book titles, and I've started and restarted this thing three different times. The book has had a different heartbeat each and every time. So when it finally became what it is today and we were ready to pitch to publishers, it was a dream come true. I had been working hard and pushing myself deep. As someone who does a million different things and doesn't finish any of them, pitching to publishers and finally signing a deal was unheard of for me. (Look at me now!)

My first draft was due in a shorter time frame than normal for a book. I remember my agent, Tawny, asking, "Are you sure this looks like a good timeline to you? It's shorter than it usually is." I thought of all the free time I had on layovers, at hotels, or on the days I'm not flying and figured that six months was plenty of time.

In early March 2020, right after I had signed the contract and was ready to dig into the work of writing, the world suddenly shut down. The glittery feeling of signing a book deal and getting something I was so excited for out into the world quickly faded, replaced by fear, confusion, and many, many questions. I really didn't want to have a chapter talking about COVID because I know how much all of us are trying to move forward and heal from this time, but I think it's important to address it. As the seriousness of what was going on in our world progressed, I knew from the very first weeks that I was in one of the worst industries to survive what was happening and keep my job. The airline industry was among the hardest hit. Experts have said that it is going to take years for airlines to recover.

My job changed drastically and quickly. Even worse, I was living in Los Angeles where the virus was hitting hard. It was a lot to take in and process. No one could make a plan or figure anything out because our world was changing every day. In the first month of the pandemic, colleagues and the airline industry were already talking about furloughs and layoffs. No one could predict what was going to happen or when.

I spent almost five months knowing I was most likely going to get laid off temporarily, without anyone being able to confirm, deny, or give me any sort of leeway or insight about that prediction. I just had to wait and stay put. It was absolutely horrible. A lot of friends and coworkers handled the news and the waiting gracefully, but some handled it horribly. I fell into the category of handling it horribly. I took a leave from flying and sat around every day checking my phone to see if there was any news. I watched my friends lose their loved ones. I watched my world close down with no escape or update on what was going to happen. This was my worst-case scenario. No amount of planning, talking, praying, or crying made me feel okay. I didn't have a job to help me stay busy or keep my mind off things. I couldn't see my friends. I couldn't go to the gym to relieve stress. I couldn't walk outside without feeling crippled by anxiety.

I know you experienced it too; we all did. I know you understand deeply, but as someone who struggles with mental health, it just felt so heavy to me. It felt like no one was hit as hard as I was, and I couldn't get that feeling to shut off. Anxiety is a good liar, isn't it? Writing a book felt like an absolute stretch. How in the world could I have signed a book deal right before all of this and come out at the end writing pages full of kindness, courage, and hope when I wasn't feeling any of those things?

On top of all of these normal human emotions I was feeling because of a pandemic, I had fallen deeply in love. Talk about timing. Not only had I fallen in love, but I had found my person. The guy I had been waiting for all of my life. Joseph was healthy and loved me so well. I yelled at God so many times because of it too. How in the world could he let me go through all of these heavy relationships just to find my dream man at the start of a pandemic? I felt like I was giving Joseph the worst version of myself and struggled with guilt during the first days of falling in love. He seemed to be handling everything with grace and trust, and I felt like a burnt piece of toast sitting next to him. Like all of the things I had worked to get healthy in were slowly starting to fade away.

Joseph lived in Arkansas, and during quarantine we decided to camp out at his family's house there. It was a lot safer and less stressful than being by myself in Los Angeles. Those days looked like a lot of TikTok dances, puzzles, books, and staring at my laptop screen trying to get as many words out for my book as I possibly could. It was hard. I felt so burnt out, and all I was doing was sitting at home every single day. I had all the time in the world to write a book. It should have been the easiest thing, but oh no, it was not.

The more I sat in the house every day, the more things started to come up. My darkest, heaviest days all look like being glued to my bed. That's what this time felt like, and there was no end in sight. I pushed hard and strong. Even though most days we were stuck in the house, Joseph and I tried to have dates and make them creative. We would cook and turn on the fireplace on Netflix. We would drive around town and go look at nice houses that we dreamed about buying one day and eat takeout in the car.

One time when we were looking at houses, I completely lost it. I had finally reached my breaking point. I don't even remember what happened; I think I had just spent so much time trying to suppress my stress and anxiety about the unknown in my world, and I finally cracked. I shared that

I felt like all of the things I'd spent so long healing from were getting brought back up again. My environment was triggering me. I didn't feel like my healthiest self, but the only thing making me not healthy was me. I spent so much time in my head obsessing over the future of my life that it was making me forfeit the joy happening right in front of me.

The fact was, I still had a job. I could still pay my bills. I was in a beautiful relationship, and I was loved. For whatever reason, it took me a long time to let those truths be enough during all the unknowns that came with a pandemic. I spent so much time upset and angry about emotions that were coming back up that reminded me of my past. But you know what? They always do. The thing is, though, when stuff comes up from our pasts, it doesn't have to be this heavy, sad thing. We can see it as a reminder of how far we've come rather than thinking we've thrown away all of our growth. I didn't focus on getting myself back to a place of truth and love during this time. I spent time sitting in worry and anxiety, and it took a toll on me.

When we are in an unhealthy state of mind and something is brought up from our past, we most likely aren't going to respond healthily. For me, being stuck inside reminded me of those hard days I talked about earlier in the book after calling off a wedding and being glued to my bed. It was hard to quiet down those triggering feelings of being stuck inside, and I got really disappointed in myself. Had I really changed and gotten better? It was hard to believe I had during this time. I had to cling to the truth of my life and find light, help, and hope in the relationships all around me. When we are in a spot of remembering truth and love, it helps us respond to life in a healthy way.

———————

It's easy to be our own worst enemies. I learned this every day throughout the pandemic when I felt like a bully toward myself. Our minds are powerful places. It can be scary to spend too much time in them if we don't constantly remind ourselves of our truth. We have to lay down our crap, our fears, our worries, our stress, our anxieties, and ask God to scoop them up and take them. I'm not strong enough to do it on my own. I tried it for a very, very long time, friend. I tried really hard throughout the pandemic, and it ran me dry. I got to my breaking point. Do you know what Joseph told me? He told me that I was okay. He reminded me of how far I've come. He told me that just because I was feeling those heavy things didn't mean they were true. I think I not only needed to hear it from someone else but also had to dig deep to find the courage to believe it.

I started speaking truth to myself, reminding myself

of the things I knew to be true. I know who I am and how I've healed. I know who loves me and the life I have because of God's love. I spoke these truths out loud, I wrote them down to read daily, and I kept at it until the thoughts in my head didn't win all the time. I started to be kinder toward myself and replace lies with truth. When I felt like none of my words mattered enough for a book, I wrote them anyway. The truth had always been there. I had not forfeited my growth. I just had to get to a place where I really, truly believed that.

Please remember these words: you have not forfeited your growth. No matter how you feel right now as you read this, how the pandemic made you feel, or what you are carrying at this moment in time, you have grown and will grow. Even though life may feel like a question mark, you are not one. You may have a lot more bad days during these times than good, and that is okay. That's how we grow strong and full of courage. You are growing through this. Growing, growing, and growing. Remind yourself even when you don't feel like it.

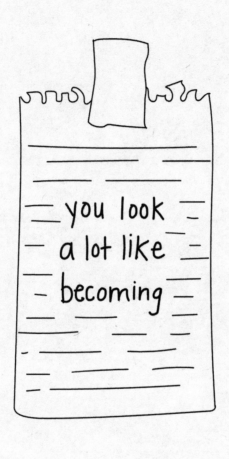

a s I write this, I'm not a flight attendant anymore. Well, I should really say that I'm not a flight attendant for the time being. In October 2020 I finally received the news that I was furloughed until my airline called me back for work. It could be less than a year or it could be five years. No one knows. It's news I dreaded hearing for six months and hoped to avoid. It's news I obsessed over and let steal my joy for way too long.

Stress is funny in that way, isn't it? Even the things we hope don't happen and stress over can happen anyway. They teach us most of the time, too, don't they? Losing my dream job is a lesson that I really would rather have avoided. But I started to realize the goodness in it, even though it's the last thing I ever wanted to happen. Losing my job in the middle of so much uncertainty going on in our world has been hard, but I think that there is still goodness and growth to be found in it. So I started to ask myself, *What could I get from this time of being away? What good is in it for me?*

I realized quickly that being a flight attendant had become my identity, and it was tiring. Not only was it my job, but it was my lifestyle, one of my biggest passions, platforms, and ways my creativity sparked. How do you have a healthy balance when so much of your life is tied to your job? As soon as someone found out what I did for work, the questions were nonstop. Don't get me wrong, I love talking about what I do and answering others' questions, but sometimes it felt like all others cared about were answers to cure their curiosity. It started to feel like the other things I could offer people were hidden behind this one, big thing. No one asked how I was or anything personal; it was just about this sparkly job I had.

Friendships have always been hard to maintain with my job as well because I'm always gone. People assume I'm out of town, or when I am in town, I need a full day to recover from work before I head right back to the skies. I miss out on a lot of birthday parties and events to support my friends. I miss out on holidays and moments to spend with my family. Even dating and finding the right person felt like an impossible mission because who would want to date someone who was never home? Relationships can be hard to build and maintain while being a flight attendant.

On top of all these things I have struggled with for the past seven-plus years, I was now in a serious relationship and starting to plan my wedding. It took a minute to dig deep, but I realized that being laid off meant a lot of time to spend with my fiancé and plan our big day. That was huge. What a time to grow and take a step back from something that had been my whole world for such a long time. I am never going to get an opportunity like this again. I am someone who has been working since I was fourteen and I never took a break. As hard as it was going to be, I was going to take this time to grow, to let go, and to prioritize all the things I never could before. I was already seeing the good and reminding myself how much I would grow because of this time.

That mindset lasted about a week though. I know myself so well it makes me laugh. Sitting around in so much uncertainty was really, really hard for me. Within the first few weeks of hearing the news of my furlough, I found a nanny job just around the corner from where I lived. I figured it would relieve me from stress about paying my bills and also keep me busy, which I thought would be good for me. I missed running around and having things to look forward to. Being around children is a double win too; they bring me so much joy. I figured I would have lots of time to prioritize all of the things that were important to me when I wasn't nannying, but it slowly became clear that I was jumping back into the same cycle of unhealthiness that flying brought me.

I came to a point where I had to decide if my need to control my financial stability was more important than my growth. Did I plan to be jobless for the whole time I was going to be laid off from flying? Absolutely not. But what if it was more important for the time being to really, truly take advantage of this time? As scary and as challenging as this time might be, who can say that they get an extended time off from their career but have confidence they will still return to it one day? I realized how special and rare this time in life will be. I had to use it to its absolute, full advantage. So, I took a deep breath and quit my nanny job. I said a lot of prayers beforehand. I had never quit a job without having another one lined up, and I most definitely knew that many people in the world were looking for jobs as well. So many people were hurting from this time. I knew how risky it was to quit a well-paying job, but I also knew how important it was to focus on things I had been putting off for years.

It was a big jump and a big risk, but becoming a better version of myself felt a lot more important than paying the bills and having some money left over. Now was the time to trust God with my whole heart and believe that I would be provided for. Please know that I'm not recommending that you quit your job. If that's what you get out of this chapter, though, and that's what you need, then you have to trust your gut. For me, I had made baby steps and big steps in my healing in order to become the healthy, whole, more-like-Love version of myself, but I hadn't done all of the work that needed to be done. I needed to learn how to be stable, to have a schedule and a routine, to go to therapy on a weekly basis, and truthfully, just to stick with something. I needed to give all of my energy and attention to becoming. To fully getting to healthiness and a me I had worked so hard to find. Saying, "This is what I am going to prioritize right now" during my time away from work meant diving in and doing the work. It meant not filling myself up with another job. It meant sitting still and being uncomfortable, and let me tell you, it hurt like absolute heck.

Waking up every day trying to make my high-energy, non-schedule-driven self comfortable with routine and relaxing was nearly impossible. I felt defeated all the time. I felt useless, untangling the years of staying busy and running around the world with no set of boundaries. I'm just supposed to sit here, read, eat healthy meals, go to therapy, work on relationships, and become the best version of myself? *Boring.* I wanted to be busy and stay rowdy so I didn't have to reflect on what was inside. This time felt a lot like the time I was walking alone in the middle of a road in Portugal. It felt as if I was dealing with the same issues of not wanting to dig deep and deal with the pain. To be honest, a lot of life and growth has felt like going around the same mountain over and over again, relearning and unlearning, until I get closer to the me I want to be. A lot of our becoming and our healing comes in waves, doesn't it? Even though I healed a lot during my time in Portugal, here I was with more to do years later.

Do you know what I am realizing though? Becoming the best version of yourself requires that we're always doing more work in order to keep looking a lot more like

Love. If we aren't looking inward and growing outward, we have work to do. Becoming the best version of yourself is a work in progress. Always. That's the beauty of this life thing. We grow and grow and grow. We get it wrong sometimes. But growth is like a flower that is withering and struggling to stay alive, then later comes back to life and blooms. We don't look at it and say, "Oh look, it's better now." We say, "Look, it's growing, and it *grew*."

Growth is this thing called grace. It's a thing called heart. It's not something we can rate on a scale of being good or bad, a one or ten, the old version or the new. It's not about being better or being worse; it's about becoming. It's about breakthroughs. It's about the heart and the guts and the fights you have late at night with yourself and the people you love. It's what you put in, and it's what you take out. I just have to be me. I have to be trying. I have to grow and fight and wrestle and hug grace with the biggest bear hug it's ever gotten. I've got to tackle it. I just have to *be*. It's as simple as that. I want to be growing. I have to remind myself that I look a lot like becoming.

No matter what job you have, how much money is in your bank account, or if you have a ring on your finger: you look a lot like becoming. If you think you haven't made it according to society's standards or if you think you are there already, remind yourself that you look a lot like becoming. Say it every day until you really, truly believe it. It is so important to remind ourselves where we are going instead of looking at where we have been.

———————

As soon as my huge, dream career was taken away from me and I didn't have an answer when people asked the "What do you do for a living?" question, I started realizing how much those things don't actually matter. All the things the world tells us we have to be in order to be important or have significance actually leave us feeling empty and worn out most days. What truly matters is who we are deep inside, if our healthiness is where it should be. If we are growing each and every day. That's the stuff that matters. The becoming stuff.

As you leave this chapter, read these words out loud with me, okay? I am loved. I am beautiful. Thank you, body, for getting me through the hard times in life. Thank you for all you've done for me and will continue to do for me. I may not feel like I have the strength, but I do. I just have to reach down and dig deep. Even though I feel messy, I'm becoming. Even though life may not look like what I thought it was going to look like, I'm becoming. I am taken care of and loved deeply. I am going to become a lot more like Love. That is simply enough.

W hen I first started flying, I would cry easily if someone snapped at me. I had a senior flight attendant, who had been flying for longer than I had been alive, pull me aside and give me some advice. She said, "You better get some alligator skin fast." I thought, *What in the world is that, and how do I find alligator skin?!* But I slowly realized what she meant. She was trying to tell me that the job would push me, and I had to have strength to do the right thing and make the right calls with my feelings put to the side. I couldn't always take everything straight to heart. I had to be willing and able to place my feelings aside and build up courage in order to be the best version of myself in the sky. It was a pretty intense goal as I am a very empathetic, understanding person. I never wanted to come off too mean, hard, or without grace. But one day I felt like I found my own kind of "alligator skin" through trial and error. Let me show you what I mean.

I was flying a longer flight from Los Angeles to Charlotte. All of the window shades on the plane were mostly closed, so it was a nice, cozy flight. Another flight attendant and I headed out on the beverage cart to start our beverage service in the main cabin. The first rows felt like they took forever, but they always do; ask any flight

attendant if they agree and I bet you they will. We finished the first rows and then moved the cart back toward the
middle rows, and that's where this story starts.

As a flight attendant who deals with hundreds of
humans a day, I can tell from a mile away when someone is not happy. It's like I can feel their energy floating
across the small metal tube. As we moved the cart back to
stop and serve new rows, I saw her, and I started praying,
"Please don't let me have to serve this woman; she is going
to chew me out." I could just feel it.

Lo and behold, my shiny metal cart stopped right in
front of her row. I asked the person in the window seat,
middle seat, and then the aisle seat where she was sitting what I could offer them to drink. She immediately
answered with an attitude, gave me her drink order, and
also said that she had a coupon for two free drinks. Well,
in my seven years of flying, I had never had a passenger
try to give me a coupon for free drinks, and I knew that it
was not a real thing. The coupons must have been fake or
years expired. So I kindly told her, "Ma'am, I am so sorry,
but we don't take coupons here at this airline."

When I say she snapped on me, I mean she snapped
on me. She was ready for it. She started yelling loudly,
telling me how on her last flight, the flight attendants
said the same thing, but when she called customer service, they said she could use it. The story went on and on.
She was aggressively yelling at me at one point and was

also crying at the same time. I started to get very upset. She decided on water instead but was still yelling at me about the coupon. Not only was it disrespectful, but her response toward me was also not allowed. I was in the middle of trying to serve the next row, and she kept going on and on and wouldn't stop yelling at me, so I just tuned it out. It had been a long day already, and I didn't have the time to explain myself to an angry woman who wasn't going to take no for an answer.

I didn't have a lot of grace, that's for sure. I know I didn't. We moved the cart, and I could finally breathe again and take some time to let the stress run off. Situations like these are always so hard to know how to handle. But you know what? They happen every single day as a flight attendant. I'm not kidding; at least on one flight a day I have had a passenger yell at me, get an attitude when I kindly asked them to follow the rules, or just board with anger and take it out on me or another flight attendant. It's really hard being a flight attendant and loving people. It's stretching and exhausting.

Oftentimes, especially after all the trauma and heartbreak I have been through in my personal life over the course of my career, I find myself not leaving my pain at the airplane door before I show up to work. I know for a fact that I have been rude to passengers or not given them that grace I speak so highly of because of where I have been in my own personal life. There have been coworkers who have driven me absolutely crazy because our personalities didn't match or I didn't like the way they worked. Instead of having patience with them, I was snappy.

When my book agent, Tawny, first suggested that a strong focus in this book should be kindness, I felt guilty. I thought of all the passengers who may pick up this book outside of their gate at the airport and what they might think if they find out the snappy flight attendant from a past flight was the one who wrote it. I thought of a few colleagues who I really bumped heads with or wasn't as kind to as I could have been, and I felt sad. I thought back to the passenger who tore me to shreds because I wouldn't accept her coupon. Do you know what I did after I had a minute in the back to collect myself and remind myself of what I am called to? I walked all the way back to her seat, got on her level, touched her hand, and said, "Ma'am, I am so sorry I didn't have the patience with you that you needed. It was really hard when you were yelling at me in front of passengers. Let me explain so you can be reassured."

She started crying hard then and explained what was going on in her life. She apologized deeply, and we had a moment together. She ended up asking for my name so she could email my manager and send a thank-you. She really appreciated how patient I was. Let me tell you, it took guts walking back and saying sorry even when I felt like someone else needed to apologize to me. I've learned this special kind of patience and understanding throughout my years as a flight attendant.

Later that day, after all the chaos with the coupon lady, I was watching a movie called *The House Bunny* in my hotel room on my layover. And, bizarrely, there was a quote in the movie that was so relevant to what I had just learned. "Kindness is love with its work boots on." Hearing those words felt like hearing something I had long needed and searched for.

––––––––

Being a God-loving, healthiness-chasing flight attendant is extremely, extremely hard. Loving the hardest kinds of people while also being the boss and rule enforcer is really, really hard. It took me way too long to figure out the grace, love, and truth rule. There can be no truth without grace and love, and no grace and love without truth. Boundaries became my best friend. It took years to finally figure out how to enforce responsibility, leadership, and safety while having grace and love for the hard moments too. *Kindness is love with its work boots on.* I already know how to love pretty dang well if I say so myself, so hearing that kindness is simply love, with some deeper work and cooler shoes, made things easier for me. I painted kindness as a lot of different things, but I never truly thought about it as an extension of love. What a beautiful, fresh way to look at things.

Maybe you aren't a flight attendant who sits up in a metal tube all day with random humans getting upset at you over luggage and leg space. Maybe you are a parent, a freelancer, an Uber driver, a teacher, a doctor, a customer waiting in line, a passenger waiting to board the plane, or a student still in school. Wherever you are or whatever you do, I know for a fact that unkind humans inconvenience you often. Probably even daily. Do you find yourself snapping back quickly or getting easily upset? I know for a long time I have and I did. It took me years to find the secret recipe and balance. This quote is it. I find myself saying it in my head as someone is yelling at me or taking out their own life issues on me. *Kindness is love with its work boots on.* I'm challenging you now to do the same. If you don't want to do the work, maybe getting fitted for a pair of work boots isn't for you. If you are ready, though, why don't you start by looking at the person who is unkind to you differently the next time? Lace up those boots, grit your teeth, bite your tongue, do whatever you've got to do long enough to say those words to yourself. Plus, I think you look a lot better in work boots, if I do say so myself.

———

As we wrap up our time together, I really wanted to end my stories of courage and how I found my true self on a note of kindness. As I write this, we've stepped into 2021, and goodness, do we need kindness now more than ever. Not just the empty Instagram story quote kind of kindness, but the deep, life-changing, hard-work, lacing up our work boots kind of kindness. Every single day we must choose it. I look around and see so much heaviness and brokenness, but I also see it as a time to wake up and dig deep every day. To be Love and to stretch our courage now more than ever. As we walk away from growing together, I hope my words stick like glue. I hope you have learned a thing or two. I hope you feel less alone and more hopeful. My stories of failing, heaviness, growing, rebuilding, and learning are all here so that you may dig deep and choose courage for your life as well. Our time together has been so much more than simply sticking notes on airplane windows, I hope you feel it too. I am so thankful for this project I started and how it has led me here, straight to you. Our words are so important. Let's not forget it.

acknowledgments

i have so many people to thank. Thank you to my team at Thomas Nelson for believing in me. Thank you to my agent, Tawny, for sticking with me, even when I didn't email you back for three months. You are an incredible friend and agent, and the book wouldn't be what it is without you. Thank you to Elizabeth Moore and your magical email. It came at just the right time; without reading it, I would have given up on the book years ago. Thank you for being a guardian angel and my cheerleader.

Thank you to my family. Amy, you have done such a beautiful job raising us four kids. Thank you for stepping up and filling such a huge role in my life. Dad, thank you for always providing for us and being there for me the best way you knew how. I carry your soft spirit with me daily, and I'm proud to call you my father. To my siblings, I hope I make you proud. I'm sorry I'm miles away, but I carry your love with me everywhere I go. You are all bright, beautiful lights. I am proud to be your sister. And to Marni, you are my rock. I wouldn't be my feisty self without your love and protection.

To all my other family members, thank you for loving me and supporting me even though I am horrible at phone calls and distance. Grandma Alice, Grandma and Pawpaw Tippett, Papa Wayne and Eileen, Mimi and Pop-Pop, Aunt Steph and Eden, Aunt Cissy, and the whole bunch. And to the whole family I gained through loving Joseph, thank you for loving me as one of your own. I'm so glad I get to be a part of your family now too.

To my thousands of followers, fans, supporters, and readers who have been pushing me to get these words onto paper: I wouldn't be here without you. Thank you for your millions of comments and emails, always showering me with an abundant amount of kind words and support. You are the heart behind what I do. You are the reason why these words are here. Thank you to all of you, especially those who have stuck with me for years and walked with me through the strongest storms. Thank you for sharing your stories with me, helping me feel so much less alone, and entrusting me enough to help you carry the load. I really love each and every one of you deeply.

To my close group of friends: Ashley, thank you for all of the laughter. You have brought me through some of my darkest times. Your friendship means more to me than I could ever have words for. Kenz, thank you for showing up with FLAMIN' HOT Cheetos and love for me over and over again in our Chicago days. For being there through so many rough breakups and not taking no for an answer until my front door was open. For letting me live in your room and steal your toothbrush when I didn't have the strength to be alone. Thank you to Kaylie as well. You got me through so much. Harris, Courtney, Kaitlyn, Gina, Robby, Emwhen, Bryce, Abe, Adriana, Claire, Matt, Jordan, Bailey, Adrian, Savannah, Leni, Jessi, Kelby, Alex, Addy, Zilah, Johnny, Jess, Shaun, Katie, and so many other friends, thank you for your light in my life. You make me a lot more like Love. I wouldn't be who I am without you. That is big.

Last but not least, thank you to my husband, Joseph. My sweet guy. I still can't believe you are my partner for life. You are all I needed but never knew existed. Thank you for your grace, your love, your songs, your patience, your unwavering kindness, and for being you. I never knew a love like this could be mine. I will cherish and fight for you every day. Thank you for believing in my stories and broken parts. You are half of this book, and I truly wouldn't have pushed deep to write this without your love motivating me every day. I hope our kids will be proud when they pick this up off of our color-coordinated shelf one day.

All of my love to every last soul that has touched my life and made me the woman I am today. This book is here because of you, and for that I thank you.

resources

e ven in the midst of such heaviness and darkness, I had many beautiful things, people, and resources in my life to help me heal. I'm not an expert, but some of these helped me, and it would be my absolute joy to share them with you, too, in hopes that they can get you through your good days, bad days, darkest days, and all of the others in between. Let's start with the most important:

If you are feeling like life is not worth living, or if you are struggling with suicide in any way, please call the National Suicide Prevention Hotline at 800-273-8255 or visit https://suicidepreventionlifeline.org.

I talk a little bit about abusive relationships in this book. If that was too close to home, or if you need help with domestic abuse, please call the National Domestic

Violence Hotline at 800-799-7233 or visit https://www
.thehotline.org.

I cannot advocate for therapy enough. To find a therapist
who fits your needs, visit https://www.psychologytoday
.com or ask the people you trust if they have any recom-
mendations. If you have health insurance, you can find
information on your provider's website. If you don't
have health insurance, that's okay too. There are other
incredible resources out there. You can visit https://www
.crisistextline.org to connect with a counselor for free
anytime. PS: going to therapy doesn't mean you are broken; it means you are brave and strong enough to become
the healthiest version of yourself. That's something to
celebrate and not be ashamed of.

On my hardest, most painful days, the last thing I wanted
to do was get up and do something to make myself feel
better. My apartment felt like a sinking hole I just couldn't
pull myself out of. It took me a really long time to figure
out what made me feel joy, and I would like to share a
few of those joy-giving things with you. Let's start with
some books I swear by:

- ***Love Does by Bob Goff*** is what I consider the
  modern-day Bible. It is so important. Bob has this

way of challenging you yet loving you well. I feel like I'm at Disneyland when I read his books. His stories are full of whimsy and this infectious hope that only Bob has a way of giving through his words. He is a superhero to me. His book *Everybody, Always* is pretty incredible too.

- *The Harry Potter series by J. K. Rowling*—need I say more? I already shared my love for Harry Potter in an earlier chapter, but let me tell you, there is something magical about this series (no pun intended). When I felt like I didn't have anyone on my darkest days, I had Harry, Ron, Hermione, and so many other characters from this series to call friends. If you have seen the movies, that doesn't count. You have to read all of the books. I pinkie promise.

- *There I Am by Ruthie Lindsey* is beautiful to me. Not only is she a sweet friend, but she is someone whom I admire and look up to immensely. In her debut novel, she shares her personal story of a traumatic car accident that kept her in physical pain and trauma for years. Eventually, her marriage crumbled and so did she; but not for long. This book is Ruthie's story of how she got up and chose beauty, even in the midst of pain.

- *The Nightingale and The Great Alone by Kristin Hannah.* Sometimes when you are sad, sad things make you feel understood, you know? Both of these books by Kristin Hannah are incredible. They are those beautiful-yet-heartbreaking kinds of love stories.

———

Next up, hobbies. Some of these require a shower and getting out of your sleep clothes. Some days that will feel like a piece of cake, and other days that will feel like rocket science. Guess what? *That is okay!* Becoming the healthiest versions of ourselves takes courage and guts. We won't get it right every day, but when we do, goodness, will it be worth it.

- *Rock Climbing.* Listen up: I do not like gyms! I do not like using machines or working out. If that is your cup of tea, that is amazing. Go do that. I know you have heard it thousands of times before, but working out raises our endorphins, and when our endorphins are happy, it makes us happy. I found my sweet spot, and that is rock climbing. It is so much fun and the most incredible workout. I can be at the climbing gym for three hours and feel like it has only been thirty minutes. Also, the climbing community is one of the friendliest, most amazing groups of people I've ever met. I make new climbing friends every single time I go to the gym. And if you don't want to talk to anyone, that's okay too. Put on your headphones, and not a soul will bother you. If you don't have any gear, you can rent all you need at most gyms. I can't recommend climbing enough.

- *Going on a walk to get coffee.* Anyone can go on a walk, and anyone can get coffee, but going on an intentional walk for coffee is a totally different ball-game, let me tell you. Put on your favorite podcast or music and have a moment for yourself. Treat yourself with a coffee or tea, or if you hate those things, get a burger—who cares! You deserve it. Whatever kind of adventure walk you want to go on, go do that.

- *Thrifting.* Is it trendy? Maybe. Is it better for our environment? Absolutely. Is it one of my favorite things to do on this earth? Yeah! Talk about an adventure. The harder you hunt, the better the reward.

- *Writing.* Do it when you are mad. Do it when you are happy. Do it to remember or do it when you need to forget. All of the time, write it down. Get it out. The longer it stays inside of you, the more power it has. If you think you can't write, that's okay. Not everything has to be a piece of art or a prize-winning poem. Your words make you, you.

Write as much as you can and as often as you can. Let your pen be your friend. Start on the notes app on your phone; you don't need anything fancy. Just get the words out.

- **Grocery shopping at Trader Joe's.** If you don't have a Trader Joe's, I am sorry for a lot of reasons. Maybe consider moving just to be in a place that has one? Kidding (only a little). Wherever you want to go, find your favorite grocery store. Mine is Trader Joe's. Cook a meal for yourself. Don't cook a meal that you make five times a week either. Try something new. The foods we put in our bodies can affect our energy and mental health. Take care of your health too!

Did you know that dancing cured almost 100 percent of my sadness on the hardest nights? Only when I had the courage to get up, turn on some music, and let it all loose did I start feeling better. Here are a few artists and albums that I hope will heal your deepest wounds. Just put some headphones on or roll your windows down and let the breeze in while your volume is louder than your pain.

Maggie Rogers's album *Heard It in a Past Life*. Listen to the whole thing with a glass of red wine and your headphones on. I cried, danced, laughed, air punched. You name it, I did it. This album is so special and so needed. The song "Back in My Body" is unreal. I still don't think I've recovered from listening to it.

Some special songs feel like magic. I can't explain it, but when I listen to them, I just want to feel alive. They make me feel awake and hopeful and are best listened to with the windows down and the sun shining on your skin. Here are a few:

- "Wonder" by Shawn Mendes
- "Good Days" by SZA
- "Anyone" by Justin Bieber
- "Hummed Low" by Odessa
- "To Build a Home" by The Cinematic Orchestra
- "Sun" by Sleeping at Last

My husband, Joseph Tilley, also makes music. He wrote many of his songs about us and our love, and it wouldn't feel right not to put him on this list. If you want some sappy pop songs filled with a lot of love, go listen to him. "Together" is my personal favorite.

———

Please remember, healing doesn't look the same for everybody. Healing doesn't only have to happen with prescription meds, doctors, therapy, or coaching. While all of these amazing things have helped me get to the best version of myself, they are not the only way. Coffee is healing. Walking is healing. Books are healing. Friends are healing. Cheeseburgers are healing. Give yourself grace and time to become who you need to be. I'm twenty-eight and still healing from trauma, but that's okay. I'm committed to the inner work of becoming healthy and a lot more like Love. I hope these things that I have shared can help you as they've helped me on my journey. Remember, your anxiety and sadness don't get to win. We have to fight for those better, more beautiful days. They are right in front of you, my friend. Pinkie promise.

PS: I really do try to answer emails and direct messages as often as I can. I didn't feel like I had a lot of people to talk to growing up, and I never want anyone to feel that way. If you want to talk, please reach out. You can find me at @taylortippett over on Instagram. We are really good friends now, just so you know.

about the author

taylor tippett is a wildflower, adventuring around as a flight attendant. Although Taylor's day job is a flight attendant for a major airline, at her core she is a writer, dreamer, and life enthusiast.

She is a prominent social media figure who shares her travels, photos, lifestyle, photo series project "Words from the Window Seat," and other work online. Known nationally as the flight attendant who leaves random notes to make peoples' day, Taylor's acts of kindness have received recognition from *HuffPo*, Instagram, ABC News, Discovery Channel, *TIME*, and others.

When not living out of her suitcase, Taylor lives full time with her husband Joseph and sweet dog Howdy in Los Angeles. She enjoys dance parties, Justin Bieber, and her wide collection of houseplants that by God's grace are still alive. This is her first book.